Questions and Answers

on Monetary Economics

Jennie Hawthorne

Woodhead-Faulkner · Cambridge

Published by Woodhead-Faulkner Ltd
Fitzwilliam House, 32 Trumpington Street, Cambridge CB2 1QY, England
and
51 Washington Street, Dover, NH 03820, USA

First published 1984
© Jennie Hawthorne 1984
ISBN 0 85941 274 1

Library of Congress Cataloging in Publication Data
Hawthorne, Jennie.
Questions and answers on monetary economics.
1. Money – Examinations, questions, etc. 2. Money – Great Britain –
Examinations, questions, etc. I. Title.
HG221.H328 1984 332.4'076 84-51011
ISBN 0-85941-274-1 (paper)

Designed by Geoff Green
Typeset by Hands Fotoset, Leicester, England
Printed in Great Britain by St Edmundsbury Press, Bury St Edmunds, Suffolk

Preface

This revision guide has been written for all those students taking examinations with a banking/monetary/investment option. It lists questions typical of those that have been set in the Monetary Economics examination of the Institute of Bankers, together with suggested 'model' answers.

Questions are grouped in topics and preceded by descriptive notes. The relative number of questions for each topic indicates the frequency with which such questions (or topics) have appeared in banking examination papers during recent years.

The answers should be read in conjunction with current financial and business news, for even the most up to date textbook cannot keep abreast of monetary crises that change the banking scene overnight.

The division of the book into 12 topics allows teachers and students to spread the subject areas over two or three terms, to match varying examination dates.

Jennie Hawthorne
April 1984

Contents

Topic 1

The Concept of Money

The nature and functions of money and liquidity. The composition of the money stock. Alternative measures of money and liquidity in a modern economy (and in the United Kingdom in particular).

This section needs definitions and some theory. What is money? Why are some financial assets, such as bank deposits, classed as money, while others, such as Stock Exchange investments, are not? How is the quantity of money defined? 'There is no single definition of money' asserts the *Bank of England Quarterly Bulletin* December 1982 as a preface to an article on the composition of monetary and liquidity aggregates. The article explains that there are many liquid assets, which, though not included in conventional definitions of monetary aggregates, must be taken into account when interpreting monetary conditions.

The nature and functions of money and liquidity

Money is one form of wealth. It represents a claim. Real wealth consists of physical assets such as goods, machines, houses and commodities. Money claims are offset by corresponding liabilities. They are debts owed by one person or group to others who own the claim. Bank deposits are claims against the banks who hold the deposits; bank notes are claims against the Governments who issue the notes. Within a country, money claims

1

cancel out. To one group they are an asset; to another, a liability. Claims against foreigners outside a country add to that country's real wealth.

Money was once held and issued in the form of gold and silver. In times of currency crises, people distrust paper claims. They revert to holding gold and silver, whose prices rise in consequence. But normally money in the form of bank deposits, notes and coin is so acceptable in payment of debt that it can be used against anything which has a price. Bank deposits, like bank notes, can purchase, up to their nominal value, any goods and services on the market. They are liquid assets. They give their owner purchasing power which can be used directly, without any further intermediation. This attribute of liquidity distinguishes money from all other forms of wealth.

Money can thus be defined as anything that is immediately acceptable in payment of debt. Money is the good or commodity used in exchange; liquidity is its characteristic.

Functions of money

By giving its owner purchasing power, money acts as a medium of exchange. It allows goods and services to be offered and accepted at a price. Selling and buying become two separate transactions. The seller gets money; the buyer, goods or services. This is a great advantage over barter, where the buying and selling of goods must take place together ('a coincidence of wants').

Money also acts as a store of liquid wealth which can be kept until required; as a unit of account by which value can be measured in price terms; and as a standard of deferred payments, so that obligations undertaken today may be paid for tomorrow.

Any commodity, no matter what its guise, which performs these functions of a medium of exchange, a store of liquid wealth, a unit of account and a standard of deferred payments, is acting as money. If it lacks one or more of the functions, it is often classed as 'quasi money'. In order to perform the functions of money, a commodity must be acceptable as such. It is made more acceptable by being portable, fairly scarce, divisible, homogeneous, recognisable and durable.

The composition of the money stock

The composition of the money stock (money supply) means the

sum of those claims used in a country to fulfil the functions of money. The supply of money may also be called the 'stock'. The former term is generally used when referring to money creation. The 'stock' refers to the level or quantity of money. Changes in the stock outstanding do not always equal flows in the supply; for example, coin may be written off as lost. The reason for identifying the components of the money stock is for purposes of control. If Governments wish to control money's function as a store of value, they will include in their money supply definition bank deposit accounts, and similar savings, such as building society deposits. If money's function as a medium of exchange is regarded as important, then current accounts will be included in the money supply definition.

Domestic credit expansion

A country's balance of payments can affect the size of its money supply. For this reason a concept of money supply was devised in the United Kingdom which made an allowance for balance of payment flows. Known as domestic credit expansion (DCE) it showed how much increases in the money supply were caused by external transactions. A balance of payments surplus was deducted from the money supply; a balance of payments deficit added on. Thus, a concept of money supply was arrived at which excluded the impact of balance of payments transactions. DCE had two main components: (a) the increase in banking sector and overseas lending to the UK public sector and (b) the increase in bank lending in sterling to the private sector. Bank lending in sterling to overseas residents was also included in DCE because it financed UK exports and had the same domestic effect as direct bank lending to a UK exporter.

In 1982 the Government wanted a money supply measure that might forecast price rises more accurately than the money supply figures then currently in use. The Bank of England introduced M2, which focused on deposits likely to be used as transactions balances. This comprised notes and coin plus current accounts, and other private sector bank deposits under £100,000 which could be withdrawn within one month. By categorising deposits according to size and maturity, the monetary authorities hoped to identify the part of the money supply that was directly related to transactions in goods and services. Furthermore, M2 was likely to be less sensitive to interest rate changes than Sterling M3 (£M3). (*See* Table 1.)

Table 1: The money supply and money stock

The narrow definition of the money supply (M1) comprises notes and coin in circulation, plus private sector sight deposits (current accounts) in sterling.

The broad definition (Sterling M3) comprises the narrow definition plus time deposits (private sector) in sterling. Bank till money (notes and coin in circulation with the public) plus banks' operational deposits (i.e., those extra to the cash ratio) held at the Bank of England are referred to as the 'wide monetary base' (MO).

Fuller explanation of UK money stock definitions:

      Notes and coin in circulation with the public
      plus
      private sector non-interest-bearing sterling sight bank deposits
      = (a)   *the non-interest-bearing component of M1.*

M1 = (a)   plus
              private sector interest-bearing sterling sight bank deposits.

M2 = (a)   plus
              private sector interest-bearing retail sterling bank deposits.

PSL1 (Private Sector Liquidity 1)
    = M1 plus
        (b)   private sector sterling time bank deposits with an original
             maturity of up to two years
             plus
        (c)   private sector holdings of sterling certificates of deposit
             plus
        (d)   private sector holdings of money market instruments
             (bank bills, Treasury bills, local authority deposits) and
             certificates of tax deposits.

PSL2 (Private Sector Liquidity 2)
    =PSL1 plus
             private sector holdings of building society deposits
             (excluding term shares and SAYE), and national savings
             instruments (excluding certificates, SAYE and other
             longer-term deposits)
             minus
             building society holdings of money market instruments
             and bank deposits, etc.

Sterling M3
    = M1 plus
      (b) plus
      (c) plus
             private sector sterling time bank deposits with an original
             maturity over two years.

M3 =   Sterling M3 plus
             foreign currency bank deposits of private sector.

Changes in the money stock

The money stock grows through increases in the public sector borrowing requirement, and increases in bank lending in sterling to the private and overseas sectors. Money supply falls are due to increases in external and foreign currency finance, purchases of public sector debt by the non-bank private sector, and increases in the non-deposit liabilities of banks, e.g., capital or reserves.

Examples of money stock definitions in other countries

Nigeria: 'Total monetary liabilities' comprises money supply plus quasi money. The money supply itself is made up of demand deposits plus currency outside banks.

Malaysia: 'Private sector liquidity' comprises money supply plus quasi money. The money supply is made up of currency held by the private sector and the demand deposits of the private sector. Quasi money is made up of fixed savings and other deposits of the private sector.

The United States of America: This changed its methods of measuring money supply in 1980. The old measures concentrated on money within the banking system. But important changes in financial techniques meant that there were many non-banking institutions such as money market mutual funds which were not included in the money supply. The altered definitions took these into account.

M1A comprises currency plus demand deposits, minus deposits held by foreign banks and official institutions. M1B is the broader definition. It comprises M1A, plus all deposits by foreign banks and official institutions in United States building societies, current accounts and other financial institutions. M2 comprises M1B, plus all savings accounts, plus overnight Eurodollars and money market mutual funds. M3 includes M2 plus large denomination time deposits at all institutions. Figures for the total financial liquidity of the economy are published monthly along with M2 and M3. M1A and M1B are published more often.

Questions on the concept of money

Q1.(a) What are the functions of money and in what circumstances does it fail to fulfil them?

(b) Explain, in non-technical terms, what is understood by 'index-linking of financial assets'.

A1.(a) The functions of money are to act as a medium of exchange, a store of liquid wealth (value), a unit of account and a standard for deferred payments. To these 'static' functions another is sometimes added: a 'dynamic' role in guiding the economy. In its function as a medium of exchange, money avoids the 'coincidence of wants' inherent in barter. In its function as a store of value, money can be held in liquid form until it is to be spent. It can also be exchanged for future delivery contracts, and so act as a standard for deferred payments.

Money fails to fulfil all these functions during periods of rapidly changing prices (inflation/deflation). During a severe inflation, the value of money falls rapidly. More is spent and more quickly. Money no longer acts as an efficient exchange mechanism. Rapidly rising prices lessen the desire to save. Assets other than money, e.g., land, houses and paintings, function better as a store of value. Planning and long-term forecasting become hazardous. 'Inflation accounting' is introduced. If the value of money falls rapidly during a period of inflation, it will no longer function efficiently as a unit of account, and a new unit may be introduced. Inflation also erodes the ability of money to act as a standard of deferred payments. The creditor loses and the debtor gains unless adjustments are made, e.g., higher loan/interest charges. During periods of deflation, the functions of money are similarly distorted but in the opposite direction.

(b) Financial assets are assets easily exchangeable into cash, but not always at the time and in the amounts desired by their owners. They may be 'marketable' (i.e., saleable to other people). Examples are equities and gilts. They may be non-marketable (e.g., building society deposits, national savings certificates or premium bonds) and only able to be cashed through the organisation or institution that issued the assets. Index-linking 'links' incomes or savings to changes in the average price level. The linking is by contract or statute and ensures that the real (not the nominal) value of certain financial assets keep their value during periods of inflation. Examples of such index-linked financial assets in the United Kingdom are 'Save as You Earn' schemes and index-linked gilts.

Q2. What forms of asset are generally regarded as being money? Why are others excluded? Illustrate your answer with reference to any country with a developed monetary system.

A2. The forms of asset which are generally regarded as being money are those which possess the functions of money: that is those which serve as a medium of exchange, a store of liquid wealth (value), a unit of account and a standard for deferred payments. In the United Kingdom these assets are coin, notes and bank deposits. Assets which possess some of money's functions but not all of them include building society deposits, Treasury bills and securities not acceptable as media of exchange. Such assets are known as quasi money. Some are included in the monetary aggregates known as PSL1 and PSL2.

Q3. Discuss how far a country's money stock comprises
(a) liabilities of its central bank;
(b) liabilities of its commercial banks.
Does it usually comprise the liabilities of other financial institutions, and if not why not?

A3. A country's money stock usually comprises notes and coins in circulation and bank deposits. Different terminologies are used in different countries to define the money stock. In the United Kingdom it is MO (notes and coin in circulation with the public; banks' till money and bankers' balances at the Bank of England) plus M1 (private sector sight bank deposits). M3 is the aggregate of MO, M1 and M2 (private sector interest-bearing bank deposits) plus private sight and time deposits in sterling (sterling M3) plus foreign currency bank deposits.

The money stock thus comprises liabilities of central banks, which issue notes, and commercial banks, which hold deposits. In the United Kingdom, notes are claims against the Bank of England. Bank deposits, both sight and time, are the largest part of the United Kingdom money stock. They constitute liabilities of the banks accepting them: almost entirely the commercial banks, as the central bank has very few commercial customers. The liabilities of other financial institutions in the United Kingdom are not included in the main definitions of the money stock, because they do not possess all the functions of money, but because of their growth, claims against certain of them are now included in the public sector liquidity aggregate.

Q4. What attributes must an asset possess if it is to be considered as money?

   Note to students: Questions asking whether certain items can be classed as money, or the advantages and disadvantages of using unusual monetary standards all have to be answered in the same way: i.e., do they fulfil the functions of money? If they do not, they will generally not be acceptable in payment of debt. They will have limited purchasing power and will have to be changed into 'acceptable' money, or used only for some specific good or service.

A4. To be regarded as money, an asset must be acceptable as such. This is the prime attribute or quality of all money: its acceptability. If people cannot recognise an asset as money or if they view it with distrust, they are hardly likely to accept it in payment of debt. What makes money acceptable are certain physical qualities. It should be portable, homogeneous, divisible and durable. Scarcity ensures that its value is maintained. Recognisability also increases acceptability, and therefore money backed or issued by the state (fiat money) is, except in times of war or hyper-inflation, always more acceptable than money which is not.

Q5. Why is it difficult to provide an unambiguous definition of the money stock in a modern economy? Illustrate your answer with reference to any country with which you are familiar.

A5. It is difficult to provide an unambiguous definition of the money stock in a modern economy because there are so many liquid assets which could be included in a monetary aggregate. The main reason for defining the money stock is for the purpose of control. It is relatively easy to define and measure money used as a means of payment, less easy to measure money used as a store of value. Different kinds of money can be substituted for one another. Some assets may be just in or out of their respective monetary aggregates. Thus, a store of value money can be used for transactions, bank deposits for making payments or as a store of value. Similarly, savings in a non-bank institution are difficult to distinguish in total from deposits in banks.

   For these reasons, definitions of the money stock in the United Kingdom are subject to constant revision. M1 and sterling M3 –

comprising notes, coin and bank deposits – have been used in the United Kingdom as definitions of the money stock for many years. But these do not distinguish between money used for making payments and as a store of value. Hence other aggregates such as PSL1, PSL2 and (a new) M2 have since been introduced as monetary aggregates.

Q6. Define the measure of the money supply in the United Kingdom known as sterling M3. Explain how sterling M3 would be directly affected by each of the following:
(a) an increase in sales of gilt-edged securities by the Bank of England;
(b) the payment by companies of value-added tax;
(c) an increase in sterling bank lending to the overseas sector.

A6. The measure of the money supply in the United Kingdom known as sterling M3 consists of M1 plus private sector sterling time bank deposits and certificates of deposits. (Another definition is M3 minus foreign currency deposits of the private sector.)

(a) An increase in sales of gilt-edged securities by the Bank of England reduces sterling M3. Bank deposits are used to buy the gilts. Sales made to overseas residents or to the banking sector do not reduce £M3.

(b) The payment of value-added taxes by companies means that companies use their bank deposits to pay the Customs and Excise department. Bank deposits fall, and so public deposits rise. The end result, as in (a) above, will be less bank money for lending and (unless the Government pours back the collected VAT into the economy) a fall in sterling M3.

(c) An increase in sterling bank lending to the overseas sector has no direct effect on sterling M3. Non-residents hold sterling in their own overseas banks. This does not add to sterling M3 unless an increase in lending comes back to the United Kingdom by way of increased residents' deposits.

Q7. What are the factors that cause M3 to grow or decrease?

A7. M3 grows when assets and/or liabilities are acquired. These come from the public or private sectors. Thus, the public sector borrowing requirement increases M3, and so does bank lending in sterling to the private sector or the overseas sector. M3 is decreased by the sale of public sector debt to the non-bank private sector, by any increase in external and foreign currency finance and by any increase in the non-deposit liabilities of banks, e.g., changes in capital and reserves. The last two factors are important from the point of view of accountancy, but do not generate significant changes in the size of the money stock.

Q8.(a) How essential is money to a modern community?

(b) Ruritania is a country which has abolished money. It is reported that there are no wages and no private property and that decisions are taken by committees. What decisions must the Ruritanian Government take that in Western countries are left largely to market forces?

A8.(a) Some form of money is essential to a modern economy. Without it barter would be needed or some form of central distribution of resources. Price evaluations would have to be made, a unit of account introduced, and unless the society is going to be run on a primitive, hand-to-mouth basis, there would need to be a basis for saving and deferred payments. Money, however defined, provides these functions. It generalises purchasing power so that consumers use their choice to influence production. The 'division of labour' depends on money wages being paid; specialisation and large scale industry could not otherwise take place. Money also encourages the growth of the financial institutions essential to the savings and investment functions of a modern economy. Finally, money can be used to affect the economy and achieve desired economic ends. In these ways money is essential to a modern economy.

(b) If Ruritania has abolished money, the price mechanism will no longer give a guide as to the wishes of the community. Yet the economic problems of scarcity and choice will remain. Committees will have to decide what to produce and who will produce and consume it. As wages have been abolished, jobs will have to be allocated. The level of production and consumption must be determined without any guide from market forces, as must the level of imports and exports. Directive labour and rationing may have to take place to share out the available jobs, goods and services.

Q9. What is meant by domestic credit expansion?

A9. Domestic credit expansion is a monetary aggregate which tries to allow for changes in a country's money stock by adding to it a balance of payments deficit, or subtracting from it a balance of payments surplus. This ensures that increases in the money stock caused by increased holdings of sterling by non-residents in the United Kingdom are offset. A decrease in the money stock, caused by spending abroad, is similarly offset. In this way domestic credit expansion shows an increase or decrease of the money supply created domestically.

Topic 2

The Value of Money

The value of money and changes in demand and supply. Keynesian and monetarist theories on demand and supply. The quantity theory of money.

The value of money

Value in the modern world is usually measured in price terms. A painting by Picasso is judged to have a higher value than one by an unknown artist. It therefore sells for a higher sum. Other commodities which are similarly highly regarded will similarly rate a higher price than goods which few people want. Money is a commodity too. How then can money be valued? What is its price, if any? The value of money is rated by what it will buy; its value in exchange. The price of money is interest. Interest is the price people will pay to borrow money or the reward they expect for lending it, which is the subject of Topic 5 (Interest Rates).

Although the value of money means value in exchange, a few forms of money have 'intrinsic' value: a value which depends on their ability to satisfy a want directly. Gold coins have such an intrinsic value. The value of most kinds of money depends on their 'face' or 'nominal' value, and what that face value can buy in terms of real goods and services. Modern forms of money are claims against the individuals or organisations that issue them. Claims rely on confidence: the confidence of the claimant to be able to exchange his claims into goods and services as and when required.

The value of money is related to the size of the money stock, its velocity and the volume of goods and services available. Changes in the value of money (i.e., in its purchasing power) can be measured by indices. Thus, if the purchasing power of money in Year 1 is 100 and in Year 2 is 150, we know that the value of money (its purchasing power) has increased by 50%. A price index also indicates the value of money. Thus, if the index of prices in Year 1 is 100 and in Year 2 is 200, then the value of money in Year 2 is halved.

Changes in the value of money

The value of money rises when prices fall (deflation). The value of money falls when prices rise (inflation). Changes in the value of money have the following harmful effects on the economy:

(a) *The efficiency of money:* money cannot perform its functions efficiently as a unit of account, medium of exchange, store of value or as a standard for deferred payments.

(b) *The distribution of national income:* national income is redistributed in an arbitrary manner among creditors and debtors, entrepreneurs and wage earners.

(c) *The size of national income:* national income rises during inflation but this reflects the increase of prices/incomes, not a real rise in productivity.

(d) *The balance of payments:* expenditure on imports rises because these are cheaper than home produced goods. Earnings of foreign currency decline. Both these effects come about as a result of a fall in the domestic value of money (inflation).

Demand for money

Changes in the demand for money are influenced by income and spending patterns, interest rates, and business expectations. Changes in the demand for a particular kind of money will also depend on comparative exchange rates. The demand for money for current transactions is known as active demand. Active demand affects prices (*see* quantity theory MV= PT). The demand for money to hold for future spending is known as passive demand (*see* Keynesian liquidity theory below) and affects interest rates.

Demand for money means the demand to hold money rather than other financial assets. According to Keynes, money is held for the following reasons:

(a) *Transaction*, i.e., for spending before the receipt of the next income increment.

(b) *Precaution*, i.e., as a fund for future emergencies.

(c) *Speculation*, i.e., for taking advantage of changes in interest rates on the value of financial assets.

The transactions and precautionary motives for holding money are affected by the size of national and personal incomes and spending and income patterns. These are both fairly stable. However, changes occur much more frequently in the speculative demand for money. Money is held (demanded) for its liquidity. Interest is the reward for parting with liquidity. The cost of holding idle money balances (e.g., in a non-interest bearing current account) is the interest foregone. Thus, other things being equal, demand for money falls when interest rates are high; demand for money rises when interest rates are low.

Supply of money

This is influenced by the state of the economy and Government policy. The Government, as the biggest spender, is largely responsible for increases or decreases in the supply of money. Inflows from abroad can also increase the supply of money; outflows decrease them.

Demand for and supply of money: the Keynesian analysis

(*See also* Topic 3: Aspects of Monetary Theory.) In Keynesian theory, the rate of interest is in equilibrium when the demand for money equals the supply of money. Total money demand is outside the immediate control of the Government, but the Government can increase or decrease money supply. If public sector disbursements, such as payments for social security or Government contracts, exceed receipts, such as taxes from the private sector, the bank accounts of the latter increase. Money supply rises unless offsetting transactions take place, such as outflows of foreign exchange reserves or sales of public sector debt to the non-bank public. Any shortfall between receipts and expenditure not covered by such offsetting transactions is filled by the issue of currency or by borrowing from the banking system. This borrowing is done mainly through the sale of Treasury bills, which alter the composition of the banks' assets.

Keynesians suggest that as a result of this increase in the money supply, transactors have excess money balances. The balances are reduced by the purchase of a narrow range of liquid assets such as bonds. Bond prices rise; yields fall. There is now a disparity between the old and new cost of financing capital investment and its return. Investment will be stimulated. Renewed economic activity will occur through the multiplier process (*see* pages 28-29). A common secondary effect is that the wealth of bond holders increases. In spite of the renewed economic activity, interest rates cannot fall quickly enough to ensure equilibrium between saving and investment. Fluctuations in national income must be used through the Budget to deflate (stimulate) the economy. Monetary policy is not enough.

Demand for and supply of money: the Monetarist analysis

The Monetarist theory is similar up to a point. It, too, emphasises money supply and disregards demand. But whereas the Keynesians assume that an increase in money supply will cause transactors to buy bonds with their excess balances, the Monetarists assume that an increase in money supply will cause an increase in all purchases, not merely of bonds. Increased balances (according to Monetarists) have a direct impact on the purchase of goods, services and economic activity. Increased balances (according to Keynesians) have an indirect effect on prices and economic activity, through changes in interest rates. These are insufficient to equate saving and investment at the full employment level, so fiscal (Budget) changes must be used to regulate the economy. Some economists aver that increases in money supply are caused by rising prices. If wages go up beyond productivity, part at least of these rises will be passed on to the consumer.

The quantity theory of money

The value of money is determined by what it can buy in real goods and services. Many economists believe that the quantity of money in an economy is the main influence on the price level. These economists include Locke, Hume, Ricardo and John Stuart Mill. Irving Fisher (1867–1947) popularised this 'quantity theory' by his famous equation of exchange $MV = PT$ ($M \times V = P \times T$). If the quantity of money in a community is £10,000, and the total value of all sales is £50,000, it means that the quantity of money has been used five times to get a total purchasing power of £50,000. To the money stock, Fisher gave the term M. To the number of times it was used for sales, he gave the term V for velocity. Therefore, $MV =$ the total value of all sales, including financial transactions such as the purchase of bonds, bills and shares. This totality MV can be looked at from another view-point: the number of transactions and the average price of each. To the former, Fisher gave the term T, to the latter, the term P. PT = the total value of all sales. Thus, MV (the total value of all purchases) = PT (the total value of all sales).

The difficulty with Fisher's Theory of Exchange was that M, V and T were defined as indices and P as the prices of transactions measured in base year prices. M, V, P and T all used the same base year. This meant that it was statistically difficult to get an accurate measure of V and T. As a result, a new version of the theory of exchange was formulated. It related the stock of money to the flow of income and led to new ideas about the demand for money. The 'Cambridge' equation, as the new version of Fisher's theory came to be known, takes the form of the quantity of national output and the average price of the 'final' price that makes it up. Final price means the end price after all intermediate transactions have been eliminated. Thus, the final price of a loaf of bread ignores the intermediate values of wheat, flour, etc., and takes only the final price in the market. Purely financial transactions, such as share purchases, are excluded from the Cambridge equation.

The average of the prices of the goods and services which make up the total output is termed p (to distinguish it from the P of Fisher's equations). The national output, though normally quoted in money terms is given in this equation a numerical value denoted by the term R. We then get pR = the actual quantity of final goods and services (R) multiplied by their price (p). pR is another way of defining national income in money terms. If the total value pR is divided by the quantity of money used to purchase R, we get the number of times the money stock 'changed hands', i.e., its velocity. This is termed the income velocity of circulation and is given the letters Vy. The Cambridge version of the Quantity Theory is expressed thus: M (money stock) × p (average price) × Vy (income velocity of circulation) = R (the quantity of final goods and services) × p (their average price). It tells us that national income equals the quantity of money multiplied by the income velocity of money.

In both versions, if V and T are constant (Fisher equation) or Vy and R are constant (Cambridge equation), then any change in M must lead to a corresponding change in P or p. But the Cambridge equation led on to a theory of demand for money:

namely that the demand for money is a function of income measured in current prices. The cash balances which people wish to hold will be a certain proportion of the national income. This proportion is likely to remain stable, for it depends on factors, such as the size of income, the frequency of receipts and payments and the number of households in an economy, which are constant in the short term.

This fraction of national income which people wish to hold as cash balances is termed k. Thus, $M = k(pR)$; i.e., the supply of money (M) = the demand for money (k), which is a constant proportion of national income (pR). If national income was at £40,000 and $k = \frac{1}{4}$, cash balances would be £10,000. If the quantity of money at that time was £10,000, then £40,000 would be the equilibrium value of national income. The demand for money = the supply of money = a fixed proportion (k) of national income. In the above example, if the supply of money (quantity of money) increased from £10,000 to £20,000, then either k (demand) or national income must change in response. But it has already been postulated that k is unlikely to vary in the short run. Therefore, an increase in M means that people are holding balances which are surplus to their needs. Equilibrium cannot be restored by spending more, for one man's spending is another man's income. Equilibrium can only be reached by a change in national income. When this reaches £80,000 cash balances will once more be at the right level, for $\frac{1}{4}$ of £80,000 = £20,000, the new money supply. In other words, M (the supply of money) = the demand for money $k(pR)$ = a given proportion ($\frac{1}{4}$) of a new higher national income level.

The quantity theory asserts that any increase in the money supply must affect the average level of prices, or R (the quantity of national output). If there are unused resources in the economy, then R will be most affected by an increase in the money stock. If the economy is fully employed, or the resources are inflexible, the major impact of an increase in money supply will be felt on prices. All of these consequences depend on the premise that the velocity of money remains fairly constant.

(For notes on Milton Friedman and the 'Chicago School', *see* Topic 3: Aspects of Monetary Theory.)

Questions on the value of money

Q1. Analyse how changes in the value of money affect its ability to fulfil its functions.

A1. The functions of money are to act as a medium of exchange, a store of liquid wealth, a unit of account and a standard for deferred payments. Some economists add a further function: that money plays a dynamic role in the economy. Changes in the value of money impair these functions. Thus, if prices rise fairly quickly, people will try to hold less money and more goods. The exchange value of money will have fallen in relation to the goods available for purchase.

The ability of money to act as a unit of account in price terms is eroded with changes in its value. Forecasting the cost of future projects becomes difficult and possibly hazardous for companies involved in the financing of those projects. It is also difficult to measure value in price terms, when values are altering rapidly. Changes in the value of money also affect its store of value function. If prices fall, savings will rise, for the future value of money is enhanced. If prices rise, the value of money savings falls, unless they are index-linked or interest rates compensate for the level of inflation. Commodities other than money, such as diamonds, gold, paintings, stamps, etc., will then take the place of money as a store of value. The store of value function is the first to be affected by changes in the value of money; the medium of exchange function will be the last, and may be followed by the issue of new legal tender money.

Q2. 'The value of money does not depend upon its intrinsic value.' Discuss.

A2. The fact that modern money (bank deposits, coins and notes) has no intrinsic value is proof that the value of money does not depend upon its intrinsic value. Its worth depends upon its acceptability as an exchange medium. If a coin has intrinsic value, this may help its acceptability, but this acceptability does not depend upon any intrinsic worth. Coins and notes are cheap to produce and have little, if any, intrinsic value, yet they are perfectly acceptable unless produced in excessive amounts. Then, even their nominal value may fall. Bank deposits have no intrinsic value but can be similarly devalued by the ease of their creation. An excess of any type of money tends to debase it and increase the value of any money with some intrinsic worth, such as gold coins.

Q3. Assess the significance of the speculative demand for money.

A3. The speculative demand for money is one of the three elements of the demand for money theory propounded by Keynes. It is the demand for money not to be used in the purchase of goods, nor for future emergencies, but for the purchase of financial assets. These assets are wanted as an alternative to money and are exchanged for the latter when interest rates seem likely to fall. Thus, when interest rates are high, people will prefer to hold bonds rather than have current account money in the bank, since the bonds have a yield plus the speculative hope of an increase in their price.

The Monetarists, by contrast, suggest that there is a whole range of alternatives, not merely bonds, that can be held in preference to money. Both schools of thought saw an increase in money supply causing an increase in prices, but Keynes saw this increase in the price of bonds, whereas the Monetarists saw it in a whole range of money alternatives, including consumer goods. The Keynesian analysis of the speculative demand for money is no longer quite so relevant as it once was because much of the money stock is now interest-bearing, and may well be preferred for this reason, and because of its immediate liquidity, to the holding of bonds.

Q4. What is meant by the statement that money is the measuring rod of value? With what precision can changes in the value of money itself be measured?

A4. Money can be regarded as a measuring rod of value because prices given to goods allow the value of those goods to be compared in money terms. Just as a ruler measures lengths and widths and allows comparisons of them in linear terms, money enables comparisons of value to be made in price terms. Without money, a barter system would prevail and goods be measured and exchanged against other goods.

The value of money is measured by what it can buy. This is not a very precise measure. The UK retail price index, for example, tries to calculate the value of money by reference to a basket of goods which reflect average spending patterns. But if the index contains a factor which does not affect certain individuals, then any changes in the value of money shown by the index will be incorrect as far as those individuals are concerned. Thus, if the retail price index reflects a fall in mortgage rates, or the price of television sets or cars, the value of money will only have risen for those who have a mortgage or who are about to buy a television or car. For others, the value of money may have fallen.

Topic 3

Aspects of Monetary Theory

Keynesian and Monetarist theory, including monetary and rolling targets and monetary base control.

How money influences the economy: an outline of the Keynesian and Monetarist viewpoints

Government influence on the demand for money is slight, but it can influence the money supply. If the money supply increases, transactors have balances surplus to their needs. The Keynesians believe that transactors reduce these balances by the purchase of bonds. Bond prices rise; interest rates fall. These changes are not quick or large enough to ensure equilibrium between saving and investment. Changes in national income must therefore be made to affect the economy. Monetary policy will not do.

The Monetarist analysis is similar up to a point. The Monetarists are successors to the old quantity theorists (*see* page 15). Modern Monetarists such as Milton Friedman attach even more importance to the money supply. They see it not merely as the determinant of prices but of economic activity. If the Government increases money supply through its borrowing and spending, transactors will be left with surplus balances. Up to this point, Monetarists and Keynesians go hand in hand. Now they diverge. The Monetarists claim that excess balances will be spent on all purchases; the Keynesians claim that the excess balances, if spent, will be exchanged for a narrow range of very limited liquid assets. Thus, the Monetarists see increased money supply as having a direct impact on prices and economic activity; the Keynesians an indirect effect through changes in interest rates.

The clue to the difference is that the Monetarists believe that the short-run velocity of money (the number of times money changes hands) is fairly stable. Any increase in money supply alters aggregate spending, and thus the GNP (Gross National Product), by a predictable amount. Using the quantity theory equation $MV = PT$, a change in M alters only P and/or T, because V is constant. (With full employment, an increase in T is not possible in the short run, so therefore an increase in M, since V is constant, must increase P.) One cause of an increase in money supply is when public sector payments to the private sector exceed receipts (usually taxes) from that sector. As a result of this imbalance, private sector bank deposits increase. Money supply rises. (The Government may use some offsetting transactions, e.g., sales of public sector debt to the non-bank public; or there may be outflows of foreign exchange reserves, both of which will depress money supply.)

The Monetarists assert that the increased private sector balances will be spent on goods and services. If this happens during a recession, the increased spending stimulates employment. If the economy is fully employed, the rise in GDP will be due to higher prices. GNP will rise to the point where it bears the same relationship to the augmented money supply as it had to the original money supply.

The Keynesians do not see the velocity of money as stable in the short or long run. They agree that if money supply increases, then people will have excess balances. But they may – or may not – spend the excess. (Remember the Keynesian motives for holding money.) If they do not spend the money, GNP will not be affected in spite of the increased money supply. Why? Because the velocity of money has fallen. To use the quantity theory $MV = PT$ to illustrate: any alteration in M will be compensated by a similar change in V. So, if money supply (M) increases, velocity will decrease by the same proportion. There will be no effect on P.

GNP will also not be affected by an exchange of excess balances in financial assets, such as bonds. It is only when the increased money supply lowers interest rates to the point where businessmen and consumers are induced to purchase goods and services that GNP will rise. This rise in GNP happens because the increased purchase of bonds drives up their price. They now have a lower yield. As a result, there is a disparity between the old and new cost of financing capital investment. Borrowing costs less, investment will be stimulated and there will be renewed activity through the *multiplier process* (*see* Topic 4).

The Monetarists refute this. Excess money balances lead to an adjustment in the purchase of goods and services, not just a narrow range of money substitutes. The adjustment directly affects economic activity. It was partly because of this emphasis on the transactions aspect of monetarism that the definition of 'money supply M2' was introduced. M2 identifies money (notes, coin and all deposits of the private sector under £100,000) that can be withdrawn in one month. M2 was therefore thought to be more directly related to transactions in goods and services, and less sensitive to interest rates, than any other money supply measure. The causes of an increase in the money supply are also disputed. Monetarists blame Governments for overspending. Other economists suggest that rising prices create the increased supply. If wages go up beyond productivity, part of these labour prices will be passed on to the consumer. If the Government is trying to reduce unemployment, it will let the money supply increase. Because there is a time lag between price rises and money supply changes, monetary targets are used to monitor money supply and keep its growth within certain limits or 'targets'.

Monetary targets

Monetary targets are restraints to the growth of monetary aggregates. A target used for monetary control should be fairly easy to measure, regulate and identify, be able to reflect monetary conditions and be related to the ultimate objectives of monetary (economic) policy. Some countries have targets for the narrow definition of money supply; others keep their targets trained on the broader definition. In the United Kingdom until 1982, £M3 was the chosen target. But (due to the 'corset' on and off) it did not reflect monetary conditions sufficiently accurately for control. Interest rates, the technique used to achieve the £M3 target, proved unsatisfactory. The high interest rates of 1980 did not deter firms from borrowing, and interest rates also affected exchange rates and other aspects of policy. In 1982, therefore, the new version of M2 was brought in and multiple targets of M1, £M3 and PSL2 were introduced in the Budget.

Rolling targets

A rolling target is one that is rolled over from one period to a later one in order to achieve the desired annual growth rate of money supply. Thus, if the target growth for one year is 12%, and at the end of six months growth has already reached 9%, this would mean a very stringent further three months in which money supply could not be allowed to increase by more than 3%. To avoid this 'squeeze' in the last few months, the date would be pushed forward by a total of nine months (18 months altogether). During that period, a growth of only 9% would be set. If achieved, the annual growth rate target would have been met: 9% for the first six months; 9% for a further 12 months, making the average growth rate for the 18-month period 12% per year.

Monetary base control

Since Monetarist theory declares that all inflation is due primarily to money supply growth, new methods of monetary control have therefore been considered. One such method that has been discussed is monetary base control. This means direct control of high powered money, e.g., cash, by the central bank. If all United Kingdom banks had to keep a set proportion of their deposits as reserves at the Bank of England (and/or their holdings of notes and coin), then the money supply itself would be controlled by the Bank of England. The Bank would be the source of cash, and the size of the money base would put a ceiling on bank deposit expansion. However, monetary base control has not been welcomed by the authorities on the grounds that it would lead to 'frequent and potentially massive movements in interest rates'.

Questions on aspects of monetary theory
(See also questions set on monetary policy.)

Q1. Comment on the significance of liquidity preference.

A1. Liquidity preference was a Keynesian concept, which referred to the preference for holding money, rather than any other financial asset, because of money's unique quality of liquidity (immediate purchasing power). This demand for money arises from three motives: (a) precaution – the 'rainy day' motive; (b) transactions – the need to have money to spend on everyday transactions; and (c) speculation – to hold money as a speculative asset, so that the holder can take advantage of changes in bond prices and interest rates. In order to persuade the holder of liquidity to part with money, a reward had to be offered: interest. The higher the interest rate, the greater the cost of holding money and vice versa. The concept of liquidity preference ignored the supply of money (this was in the hands of the authorities) but it emphasised the influence of expectations on the amount of money people wished to hold.

Q2. Compare and contrast the Monetarist and Keynesian viewpoints on how an increase in a country's money supply affects growth, inflation and the level of interest rates. Distinguish between short-term and long-term effects.

A2. In the short run an increase in the money supply will, according to the Monetarists, have the following effects: interest rates will fall, prices will rise and production should be stimulated by the combination of these two factors. In the long run, there will be no effect on output, and the increase in money supply will be absorbed by the higher prices, with a resultant rise in interest rates.

The Keynesian analysis is that the short-term effects of an increase in the money supply lead to a fall in interest rates and a stimulation in demand. There is some dissension among Keynesians as to whether this is an accurate scenario, because Keynes suggested that investment was interest inelastic. Investment decisions were based on factors other than interest rates. It is not also agreed among Keynesians whether increased demand would stimulate the economy or stimulate inflation. Most Keynesians believe that demand increases output until the full employment level is reached. Any increase of demand after that point lead to higher inflation.

Q3. Assess the significance of proposals to control the monetary base for the United Kingdom.

A3. In June 1979 an article on monetary base control was published in the *Bank of England Quarterly Bulletin*, and a Green Paper on the same subject came out in March 1980. The first difficulty in any effort to control the monetary base was one of definition. What should it consist of? This problem boiled down to the question of what monetary liabilities the authorities wished to control.

The monetary base, or 'high-powered money', usually refers to the total of balance sheet liabilities of the central bank to the private sector. The significance of any monetary base control is that if banks have to keep a minimum ratio of cash to deposits, and the central bank controls that source, it can impose a ceiling on the level of bank deposits and indirectly on the money supply. This form of control would involve, in extreme form, very great pressure on financial markets with little gain in the form of extra data. Though some benefits might result in the longer term, against this would have to be measured the cost of the major structural alterations that would have to take place in the financial system.

Topic 4

Saving and Investment

The trade cycle, the accelerator and the multiplier. Inflationary and deflationary gaps in an economy.

The following is a summary of saving and investment, and should help in understanding economic policy and the various alternatives a Government has in achieving certain economic ends.

The trade cycle

Consumption/investment analysis is part of macro-economics: the study of totals or aggregates. M1, M2, £M3, PSL1, PSL2 and DCE are all aggregates. Total or national income is another aggregate and one to which Keynes gave much attention. National income is the money value of the flow of goods and services produced by the work and property of a country's inhabitants in a given period of time. In a modern economy, money passes from households to firms in exchange for goods and services. The flow of money is a circular one. It passes out of firms as wages, profits, and rent, and then returns through spending on products. One man's spending is another man's income. Payments by one group are receipts by another. In other words, national income equals national expenditure. The circular flow of income/expenditure does not, however, remain static. It can rise or fall. Changes in its level affect saving, investment and employment.

Why does the level of income/expenditure change? It rises when there is more production, investment or export sales. It falls when there is more saving, taxes or imports. It is as if there are two people paying each other for various jobs. The distribution will alter but the total amount will not change, unless there is saving (one of the men decides not to buy the other's products) or the money goes out of the system (a gift to a relative overseas); or there is an injection of more goods/cash from the two partners or from outside (a gift from a relative overseas). Income is created by spending. Spending on consumer goods (those which are 'eaten up' within a year) is called Consumption (C). Spending on capital goods (those which make other goods) is called Investment (I). Spending by Governments is another form of spending (G). The circular flow of national income can grow larger by injections (J). These are additions to the income of households which do not arise from the spending of firms, and additions to the income of firms which do not arise from the spending of households. Investment adds to incomes without any change in the spending of households on goods and services. It is an injection. Exports (X) provide extra income for domestic households and firms. They are also injections, as is Government spending.

When there are withdrawals, the circular flow of income falls. Withdrawals occur when income is not passed on in the circular flow to firms through spending by households; or to households through spending by firms. Savings (S), taxes (T) and imports (M) are withdrawals. If total injections (J) exceed total withdrawals (W), total (national) income expands. If total withdrawals exceed total injections, the circular flow of income diminishes. Equilibrium occurs when injections equal withdrawals. This equilibrium need not coincide with full employment level, but it will continue until W or J alter. A rise in J will increase national income; a rise in W will reduce national income. Governments therefore have the power, through their budgets, to raise or lower the levels of national income and thus the level of employment. This Keynesian analysis appears true for deflationary periods; but not as a cure for inflation.

The accelerator

This is the principle which shows how changes in the demand for consumption goods lead to changes in capital goods at an accelerated rate. The acceleration occurs because investment in machines (capital goods) consists of replacements, as well as the purchase of extra machines to meet the higher demand. The accelerator principle also works in reverse when demand falls. Fluctuations in output and employment are therefore usually more severe in the capital goods industries than in the consumer goods industries (*see* Table 2).

Table 2: The accelerator (example)

A box factory has 50 machines. Each machine produces 400 boxes per year (total production = 20,000). 10 machines are replaced every year.

Demand for boxes	% Increase in demand	Machines used	New mach-ines needed	Total investment	Change %
Year 1 20,000	–	50	10	10	–
Year 2 24,000	20.0	60	10+10	20	100
Year 3 28,000	16.6	70	10+10	20	–
Year 4 30,000	14.0	75	05+10	15	−25

It can be seen from the table that although the demand for boxes increased from 20,000 to 24,000 in Year 2 (20% increase), the increase in gross (total) investment was 100%. The demand for machines doubled from 10 to 20.

The multiplier

Injections into the flow of national income do not raise the national income by the amount of the initial injection, but by a multiplied amount. For example, if an original injection by Government spending is £20,000, and national income thereafter rises to £40,000, we say that the multiplier is 2. The multiplier can be defined as a measure of the change in the size of national income brought about by changes in aggregate expenditure.

Income determines the level of consumption and saving. If incomes rise, a proportion of the extra income will be spent and a proportion will be saved. The proportion spent is known as the marginal propensity to consume (MPC), and the proportion saved is known as the marginal propensity to withdraw (MPW) or the marginal propensity to save (MPS). Where (W) is the extra income withdrawn from the circular flow, the multiplier equals 1/W. It is the reciprocal of the marginal propensity to withdraw/ save. By contrast, in Year 3, although demand is still increasing (4,000 more boxes are wanted, a percentage increase of 16.6% over Year 2), total investment is at the same level as the previous year. In Year 4, although demand for boxes is still increasing by 2,000 in this year (a percentage increase of 14% over Year 3), total investment actually falls by 25% from a total of 20 machines to a total of 15. An example of the multiplier process follows:

Table 3: The multiplier (example)

Assume the government spends £10m on building new roads (an injection of £10m). Road builders' incomes rise by £10m. Some part of this extra income will be saved (e.g. 1/10), the remainder spent (9/10). This £9m is passed on in the form of spending on home-produced goods and services. The people who receive this £9m will do likewise, i.e., they will save some of their increased income and spend some. If we assume they also save 1/10 and spend 9/10 there will be a further passing on of income. The process can be illustrated as follows:

National income £m	MPC 9/10	MPS (MPW) 1/10
10.0	9.0	1.0
9.0	8.1	0.9
8.1	7.29	0.81
7.29	6.561	0.729
—	—	—
—	—	—
% 100.0	90.000	10.000

MPC = marginal propensity to consume
MPS = marginal propensity to save

The inflationary and deflationary gaps

The economy is in equilibrium when injections equal withdrawals and income equals expenditure. However, the equilibrium national income may be at a point where there is unemployment of resources. A deflationary gap exists. Alternatively, equilibrium national income may be greater than full employment level. An inflationary gap exists.

Some short self-testing questions on saving and investment

1. Define macro-economics.
2. Define injections.
3. Define withdrawals.
4. Define neutral equilibrium.
5. What conditions must exist for an economy to be in neutral equilibrium?

6. What do the letters GNP and NNP stand for? (These are not given in the text.)

7. Give three types of withdrawals and state their relationship with national income.

8. Give three types of injections and state their relationship with national income.

9. What happens to national income (Y) if injections (J) exceed withdrawals (W)?

10. What happens to national income (Y) if withdrawals (W) exceed injections (J)?

11. An economy is in equilibrium. What would the effect on national income and employment levels be if there was: (a) a rise in exports (b) a fall in savings (c) an increase in Government expenditure (d) higher taxation.

12. A Government wishes to offset the following: (a) a fall in imports (b) a fall in exports (c) an increase in saving (d) a fall in investment. What taxation policy should it adopt in each of the above cases?

13. What is the multiplier?

14. Give two formulae for finding the multiplier.

15. People receive extra income, and each spend the following amounts: (a) 4/5 (b) 3/5 (c) 2/3 (d) 1 (e) 0. What is the multiplier in each case?

16. (J) exceeds (W) by £10m. The marginal propensity to withdraw is 1/10. By how much will national income (Y) increase before equilibrium is reached?

Answers to self-testing questions

1. Macro-economics is that part of economics which deals with aggregates or totals, e.g., the level of prices; the volume of employment; the money supply.

2. Injections are additions to the income of households which do not arise from the spending of firms, and additions to the income of firms which do not arise from the spending of households. They are investment, exports and Government spending.

3. Withdrawals are incomes which are not passed on in the circular flow. They are savings, imports and taxation.

4. Neutral equilibrium exists when national income is neither rising nor falling.

5. For an economy to be in a situation of neutral equilibrium, expenditure must equal income or injections must equal withdrawals.

6. GNP means Gross National Product. NNP means Net National Product. NNP is GNP minus the component of capital consumption (depreciation). Another term for NNP is national income, and in diagrams and graphs is often given the symbol (Y).

7. *See* answer to 3 above. Withdrawals rise and fall with income.

8. *See* answer to 2 above. Injections do not vary with national income.

9. National income rises.

10. National income falls.

11. Both national income and employment levels would (a) rise (b) rise (c) rise (d) fall.

12. Taxes must: (a) rise (b) fall (c) fall (d) fall. Note that the answer to (a) assumes that taxes will make home-produced goods dearer, so that imports will become cheaper and more easily bought.

13. The multiplier is the figure by which the change in injections is multiplied to find the resulting change in national income. Alternatively, it is the figure which results from national income being divided by the injections.

14. (i)

$$\frac{\text{Change in (Y)}}{\text{Change in (J)}}$$

(ii) 1/MPW

15. (a) 1/5 is the amount saved; therefore the multiplier is 1 divided by 1/5 = 5. (b) 2.5. (c) 3. (d) If people spent 1 of every 1 received then (W) = O, and the multiplier = infinity. (e) 1.

16. The multiplier = 10, therefore the increase in national income, resulting from an injection of £10m, is £10 × 10 = £100m.

Questions on saving and investment

Questions on the above topics come up regularly in exam papers set by various professional institutes and boards. They rarely appear in the Monetary Economics exam of the Institute of Bankers. It is doubtless assumed that by the time young bankers have passed all their earlier exams, they will have mastered this part of economic theory.

Q1. What factors influence the volume of investment spending on fixed assets by business firms?

A1. The factors which influence the volume of investment

spending on fixed assets are demand for the product, the level of interest rates, the returns to be derived from the projected expenditure, business expectations generally and Government policy.

Any increase in demand for a product predisposes an entrepreneur to invest in fixed assets to meet that demand, but he will only go ahead if it appears profitable to do so. When the cost of borrowing exceeds the expected return, there is little incentive to invest, at least in the short term. Long-term prospects may be different, particularly if the economy is active or showing signs of recovery.

Government policy has an important impact on investment. It affects saving and investment in many ways. Capital allowances and/or tax concessions encourage the purchase of new plant. Direct and indirect Government grants and subsidies stimulate specific areas or sectors of the economy. Thus, housing improvement grants stimulate the construction industry and thereby fixed assets for that industry. Investment grants in certain areas, rate or rent concessions on factory premises and capital allowances on plant are all examples of Government policy, the object of which is to stimulate investment. In the final analysis however, decisions to invest by business firms have to be made on the basis of profitability. Different criteria are used for investment decisions by Government.

Q2. Distinguish between the average propensity to save and the marginal propensity to save. Give reasons for any increase in the marginal propensity to save in the personal sector of the British economy.

A2. The average propensity to save is the proportion of savings to total income. Known as the savings ratio, it is the ratio of savings to personal disposable income. Disposable income is the income remaining after the deductions for direct taxation, national insurance contributions and any similar levies which come directly off the wage packet or salary.

The marginal propensity to save is the proportion of extra income that is saved and not spent. If the marginal propensity increases, so does the average propensity and vice versa, in the same kind of relationship as shown by average and marginal cost curves. The marginal propensity to save is an important concept in macro-economics. If the marginal propensity to save is 25%, that is, for every extra 100p earned 25p is spent, the multiplier equals 4 (1/MPS). Every extra unit of income received will generate, through the multiplier process, four times the amount of original expenditure.

As income increases, the amount of spending falls in relation to total income and savings rise. This can be easily understood when one thinks of the lowest income levels. At zero point and below it is impossible to save. Life itself may have to be sustained by borrowing. At the highest income levels however, it is difficult to spend all the income received. A greater proportion will be saved. It was originally thought that during periods of inflation, people would spend more, so as to preserve the purchasing power of their money when prices were rising. As inflation was accompanied by unemployment ('stagflation'), however, the precautionary motive for holding money became more important and savings increased.

Topic 5

Interest Rates

The Keynesian and classical theories of interest. The term 'structure of interest rates' and a definition of 'real' and 'nominal'. The relationship between domestic, international and Eurocurrency interest rates.

Interest

There are two ways of looking at interest. The first way is as a price for the use of a loan. The lender gives up the use of money and wants compensation for the loss of money's liquidity. This is a time theory of interest: an exchange of a claim on today's resources for a claim on tomorrow's. Compensation (interest) is wanted partly because the lender now cannot use his money even if he needs it. Interest is also wanted in case the money is lost, or if there is a fall in its value during the period of the loan. Strictly speaking, any reward for risk is profit; and any fall in the repayment value of the loan should be compensated for by insurance. But the element of liquidity is always lost and the reward, or compensation, for this loss must be regarded as pure interest.

The Keynesian (or monetary) theory of interest

Keynes saw interest as a reward for parting with liquidity. Interest was a monetary phenomenon determined by monetary forces. The interest rate was an equilibrium price between the demand and supply of money. The *supply* of money was in the control of the monetary authorities. They could increase or decrease it by their actions – budget deficits or surpluses. The *demand* for money was for its liquidity.

Interest charges do not affect the transactions and precautionary motives for holding money (*see* Topic 3). No householder is going to rush out and load up with vegetables because there has been an increase in interest rates. And the amount that people keep as a precaution for a 'rainy day' is allied to their income, not to interest rates. But speculators will alter their holdings of financial assets when interest rate changes or is expected to change. To induce people to reduce their holding of (demand for) money, a higher interest rate must be paid. The higher the interest rate, the greater is the cost of holding money; the lower the interest rate, the lower the cost of holding money. (Holding money means holding money that is immediately liquid as in a current account.)

If interest rate falls, the prospect of further falls gets less. People believe the rate must go up and so at this point they will not change their holding of money (demand) unless there is a very great fall in the interest rate. This elastic part of the demand curve is based on past events and future expectations. It varies from country to country and is known as the 'liquidity' trap. One can summarise the Keynesian (or monetary) theory of interest by saying that is a *demand* theory. The supply of money is in the control of the authorities, and so is fairly inelastic. The demand for money changes with business expectations, and with changes in the cost and reward of holding different kinds of financial assets.

The classical theory of interest

(Some text books give other names to this theory, e.g., the non-monetary, real, or loanable funds theory of interest.)

This theory shows interest as the equilibrium price between the demand for and supply of capital. Why capital, and not money as in the Keynesian approach? The different emphasis is because the classical theory does not give the same importance to liquidity. Furthermore, it is a long-term theory with interest rates bringing the forces of demand and supply into equilibrium. Keynes was not interested in long-term theories ('in the long run we are all dead'). His is a short-term theory, and one in which more emphasis is placed on the speculative demand for money.

In the classical theory of interest, the demand for capital comes from borrowers who wish to use it to make a profit. The price of the loan, interest, is balanced against the reward for using it. The entrepreneur looks at the marginal productivity of his capital. A positive result means that he or she can go ahead. He will borrow up to the point where the marginal return on a unit of capital equals the marginal cost (interest) of borrowing it. The supply of capital is not influenced by Government. It comes from savers. The amount of saving in any community depends on: (a) social influences, e.g., the development of financial institutions; the habit (or lack) of thrift; (b) the age of the population; (c) religious or similar influences which emphasise asceticism or reject conspicuous consumption; (d) the total income of the community, for rich countries can obviously save more than poor ones and the same goes for people; (e) the distribution of income; an equal distribution can mean more is being saved than when income is fairly divided; (f) technical considerations, such as the efficiency of financial institutions or the rate of interest (a higher rate may induce people to part with savings even at greater risk and inconvenience).

In the classical theory of interest, these two forces – demand for capital by borrowers (entrepreneurs) and the supply of capital by savers – have a point of intersection: the rate of interest.

The term 'structure of interest rates'

A yield is a percentage return on the market price of an interest-bearing asset. Thus, if I buy a £100 bond with an interest rate ('coupon') of 10% and I paid £100 for the bond, my yield is 10%.

$$\text{Yield} = \frac{\text{nominal value of the bond (£100)} \times \text{interest (10\%)}}{\text{market price of the bond (£100)}}$$

If the bond costs me £50, the interest rate on the bond is still fixed at 10% but my yield is now 20%.

$$\text{Yield} = \frac{\text{nominal value of the bond (£100)} \times \text{interest (10\%)}}{\text{market price of the bond (£50)}}$$

The term 'structure of interest rates' means the spread of interest rates over assets of different maturities. The yield curve summarises the term 'structure of interest rate'. It shows how the yield on a financial claim changes as the claim approaches its maturity (redemption date). The yield curve is usually upward sloping, rising with time to maturity. This reflects the demand/supply conditions for assets of different maturities. Short maturities usually have higher prices and lower yields: the demand for them is higher relative to their supply. A change in expectations about future rates alters the term structure. If there is a fall in interest rates, the price of claims (bonds) will rise, and the longer-dated claims will rise the most. This increase in demand for long-term debt causes the yield curve to slope less steeply upwards, or even to fall.

The tax position of the lender/borrower and the costs of purchasing financial assets may affect the net return to an investor. Interest rates generally rise in inverse proportion to the liquidity of an asset. Claims against the Government such as gilt-edged stock or Treasury bills are safe and liquid. But the earlier the certainty of capital repayment on a particular bond, the lower the interest rate on that bond tends to be.

'Nominal' and 'real' interest rates

A 'nominal' interest rate is the interest rate attached to the asset being bought, sold or hired. The 'real' interest rate is the nominal rate adjusted for changes in the price level. Thus, if the nominal interest rate on a bond is 8% per year, the value of the bond with interest added at the end of one year is £108. However, if prices have risen by 10% in the year, there is a loss of 2% in 'real' terms.

Relationship between domestic, international and Eurocurrency interest rates

Domestic interest rates in a country depend on the security and length of the loan, its ease of withdrawal, the collateral of the borrower and money market rates, which are influenced by the general economic situation. The size of the Government's borrowing requirement exerts strong pressure on the level of interest rates. If the Government wants to raise large sums from the general public by the sale of bonds, it will have to issue stock at sufficiently attractive yields for people to buy them. High inflation will cause the interest rate to be markedly higher than in a situation where prices are falling.

The level of interest rates abroad exerts an influence on domestic rates. Money tends to flow where the returns are greatest, affecting exchange rates. A country suffering a large deficit in its balance of payments may try to rectify the situation by raising its internal interest rates. Interest rates are also used by countries to control the money supply. This technique is imprecise, however, and may not achieve the objectives required.

Eurocurrency interest rates

A Eurocurrency is any currency operating as loan and repayment outside the country of origin. Eurocurrency interest rates follow the trend of the currency in which they are denominated (e.g., Eurodollars, Eurosterling, etc.). They are issued by intermediaries, not by a central bank, and there are no lenders of last resort facilities. For these reasons, interest rates paid on deposits in Eurocurrencies are always higher than those paid on the corresponding domestic currencies.

Questions on interest rates

Questions on interest rates are usually seeking to find out how much the student knows of interest rate *theory*. Questions on money markets (the United Kingdom financial system) are seeking answers in factual terms: base rate, deposit rate, Treasury bill rate, LIBOR, etc. Theory is used to explain why interest rates change and the relationship between domestic and other interest rates, including those of the Eurocurrency market.

Q1. Outline the main reasons for the higher levels of interest rates in recent years.
(Note to student: this question should be answered in terms of the general reasons for higher interest rates, rather than the levels in specific years.)

A1. Reasons for higher levels of interest rates include the following: (a) *Inflation*. Lenders must get a higher return on their money to induce them to lend at all. (b) *Monetary controls*. If emphasis is placed on interest rates as a method of control, rather than fiscal policy or quantitative controls (such as those existing pre-1971) interest rates will rise to make borrowing more difficult. (c) *The Government borrowing requirement*. When this is large, gilts must have high enough yields for the public to subscribe for them. (d) *Balance of payments deficits*. When there are balance of payments (or exchange rate) difficulties, interest rates may have to be raised to prevent an outflow of capital and to attract funds from abroad. (e) *Demand for capital*. Any increase in the demand for capital is likely to cause a rise in interest rates, e.g., the rate for mortgages rises when demand for house buying increases.

Q2. Discuss the factors which affect the level and pattern of money market interest rates in the United Kingdom. To what extent do changes in money market rates lead to changes in commercial banks' base rates?

A2. Interest is the price of money. For individuals, this price is affected by the term length of the loan and the collateral of the borrower. In the money market, the Bank of England's open market operations are a decisive force on the level of interest rates. Since the August 1981 measures, the Bank intervenes in the money market, not merely for smoothing operating but to influence short-term interest rates. The Bank buys or sells bills from and to the discount houses in four bands, according to their maturity dates. Any change in bands one and two (those of a maturity up to 14 days and one month respectively) suggests the Bank's intention to change the general level of interest rates. The base rate of commercial banks will move in sympathy. Longer-term rates are more influenced by the market forces of supply and demand. These forces depend on such factors as liquidity preference, the Government's borrowing requirement, inflation, exchange rates and the interest rate in other countries, particularly the United States.

A high inflation rate usually means a higher level of interest because lenders want a real rate of return. Gilt-edged securities have to offer a rate of return that will attract buyers. Short-term rates will move roughly in line with bill rates. The longer-term rate will go up or down to reflect expectations of future trends in the economy. Any worry about the exchange rate or balance of payments may mean higher interest rates to attract money from abroad. Changes in money market rates must affect the banks' base rate, i.e., the rate on which banks base their lending. Large companies usually get better rates than do private customers. If they can borrow more cheaply from the banks than in the money market, such companies will switch to bank finance ('soft arbitrage'). Bank rates cannot therefore lag too far behind rising money market rates, otherwise the large companies with bank borrowing facilities will use them to re-lend at the higher rates prevailing in the market ('hard arbitrage'). Banks thus try to link their lending to rates prevailing in the money market, which means that money market rates affect base rate fairly quickly.

Q3. State the main effects of a rise in a country's interest rates on: (a) its internal economy; (b) its banking system; and (c) its external situation.

A3. (a) The effect of high interest rates on a country's internal economy is to affect the volume of consumption. Capital investment is affected to a lesser degree as it is more interest-elastic, with the return on capital being more important than its borrowing cost. Interest rate increases have far less influence on public sector investment than do other considerations, e.g., the degree of unemployment and the current price level. Expectations of future costs and prices, including interest rates, affect the demand for long-term projects. A rise in interest rates will not deter investment in capital goods if the rate is expected to be high only for a short duration and then fall.

(b) A rise in interest rates usually increases a bank's profitability because the cost of holding current account money becomes less. A bank's portfolio of fixed interest assets will, however, lose some of its value. The overall position of the banking system depends on the amount of their current accounts, the level of interest rates and the value of their assets. If the collateral for bank advances is based on fairly illiquid assets at a given level of interest, any rise in interest rates would not only result in a fall in bank profits, but in serious cash flow and liquidity problems such as occurred during the 'fringe' banking crisis. (Since 1981 the Bank of England has set out guide lines for a cash flow approach to liquidity.) Wholesale banks depend for their profitability more on the *margins* between interest rates than on the *levels* of interest rates.

(c) A rise in a country's interest rates tends to induce a flow of capital from abroad. This increases the level of a country's reserves and improves its exchange rate. Higher interest rates have little impact on exports unless they reduce price competitiveness, but they may have some bearing on the export finance provided by banks. However, interest rates in themselves do not have as much impact on a country's external situation as do its growth rate, level of employment and degree of inflation.

Q4. What are the factors determining the pattern of interest rates allowed on deposits and charged on advances by the various types of commercial bank in the United Kingdom?
(Note to student: this question is asking for a knowledge of the various types of commercial banks in the United Kingdom. A similar question could be asked regarding the interest rates applicable to building societies or licensed deposit takers. The student would also need to explain how such institutions

determine their interest rates. The question is *not* asking for an explanation of the general level of interest rates, such as would be explained by the theory of liquidity preference.)

A4. The factors which affect the pattern of interest rates used by the retail banks are the demand for advances, the cost of maintaining expensive branch networks and the competition from other financial institutions and investment media. A sufficient margin must be kept between base and deposit rates to ensure sufficient liquidity and profitability. This margin will vary, depending on the levels of deposits and demand in any particular period, on the status of the customer and on any lending directives or monetary controls in force at the time.

Retail banks tend to link lending rates to money market rates in order to prevent arbitrage transactions by corporate customers, as the clearing banks themselves operate in the wholesale markets. American and other foreign banks in London, as well as merchant banks and licensed deposit takers, all operate in the wholesale money markets. Their operating costs in relation to their balance sheets are much smaller than those of the retail banks, so they work on narrower margins. They are more affected by the overall forces of money demand and supply. Their lending is not linked to base rate as is the case with the retail banks, but with the London inter-bank offered rate. Factors which affect all banks include competition from other lenders, deposit takers and the Government, as well as the level of economic activity.

Q5. If a bank, operating in a modern community, is free to determine its own interest rates on deposits and advances, what factors influence it in doing so? What particular considerations, if any, apply to United Kingdom banks?
(Note to student: in an exam, the *first* part of this question was allocated two-thirds of the marks.)

A5. Any bank works on the principle that it must cover its cost and make a profit on its operations. This means that it must match its demand for funds with a sufficient margin against the supply of funds. In trying to achieve this objective of overall profitability it will have to compete with other banks and financial institutions, and this factor must also be taken into account. So, too, must the discount rate of the central bank. Inflation cannot be ignored nor can the interest rates of other countries. An important consideration for United Kingdom banks is that they borrow in the wholesale markets and must beware of arbitrage transactions from their customers. Another consideration applying to United Kingdom banks is the type of Government monetary policy, or the restrictions on lending, which may be in operation at any given time.

Q6. Why, in practice, are there so many different rates of interest in a country such as the United Kingdom?
(Note to student: this is another question which should not be answered in general terms of supply and demand. Such an answer is not explicit enough, and does not account for the different levels of interest rates operating in the various markets.)

A6. In spite of Government economic policy, monetary controls, inflation and interest rates in other countries, there will still be no one uniform interest rate for all classes of loans and deposits. There are three main reasons why rates charged on loans and offered on deposits (interest rates) vary. They are risk, time and amount. The longest loans usually have the highest interest rate, but this may not always be the case. Sometimes overnight money is in extremely short supply and the rate can equal an annual rate of around 30%. In the sterling crisis of June 1972 overnight money rates went even higher.

Overdrafts, discounting and term loans all have different time and risk scales, and hence different interest rates. The risk element for banks is compensated for by their charging a margin over base rate or LIBOR. This margin will depend partly on the credit rating of the customer (with first-class risks having to pay the least), and with the cost of supplying such funds by the banks. In England, current account deposits form a larger part of the banks' deposit base than they do in Scotland and Wales.

Some institutions give special rates because of current legislation: thus, building societies are entitled to pay an interest rate to their depositors which is tax paid, because of prior arrangements with the Inland Revenue. Other institutions may offer higher rates on larger amounts or for special classes of customer. The Bank of Ireland in 1980 made special interest rates for older depositors.

The type of currency in which loans are made will have a bearing on the rate charged – this is another element of risk. Eurocurrency loans are cheaper than those in domestic markets. Finally, interest rates may not reflect market forces at all, but may be the result of legislation. (Such legislation on different types of loans and deposits operated in the United States before 1980.)

Q7. Describe the role and assess the significance of the London inter-bank offered rate LIBOR.

A7. LIBOR is the rate charged on loans between banks in London for different periods ranging from overnight loans to loans up to one year. It is a market rate influenced by the demand for and supply of funds in the market. Inter-bank lending and borrowing smoothes out the liquidity levels between banks. The three months' LIBOR is used for calculating rollover term loans in sterling. It is also now used as a base for calculating overdraft lending rates to corporate customers. LIBOR has also been used by some banks for compiling internal rates of interest so as to establish the profit and loss figures for their branches. Although LIBOR is a London-based rate, it is used too in the Eurocurrency market for calculating the rate on rollover credits and floating rate bonds.

Q8. Explain briefly in your own words and for the benefit of non-bankers the meaning of the term 'MLR'.

A8. MLR is the abbreviation used for minimum lending rate. It was once the minimum rate at which the Bank of England discounted first-class paper, or lent to the discount houses against the collateral of that paper. It could be a market rate or an administered rate. Before 1971 MLR was known as Bank rate, and the Bank of England fixed the rate in line with its policy. Competition and Credit Control came in 1971 and interest rates were left, in theory, to market forces. The minimum lending rate was therefore related to the Treasury bill rate, by adding $1/2\%$ to the latter, rounded up to the nearest $1/4\%$ above. The authorities could suspend the formula when they thought fit, as they did in 1973 when MLR was raised to 13%. In 1978 MLR was abandoned in all but name and it became an administered ('or discretionary') rate. After the monetary control measures of August 1981, the Bank of England discounted the practice of announcing a minimum lending rate at which it would lend to the market, but explained that it might wish to re-introduce the practice on a temporary basis at some future date.

Topic 6

Monetary Policy

Aims of monetary policy and its effectiveness and limitations. The change to monetary policy from fiscal policy (*see also* Topic 7). General techniques of monetary control and the influence of monetary policy on the banking system.

Definition

Monetary policy means control through the banking system of the money supply, either directly by a limit on its growth or indirectly by measures which affect the cost and availability of credit.

Aims of monetary policy

The aims of monetary policy vary at different times. During a period of rapid inflation, the main objective may be to reduce price levels. At other times, reduction of unemployment or a balance of payments surplus will be the policy goals. (*See* pages 56-57 for a comparison of monetary and fiscal policy.)

Conflict of aims

One of the tasks of the Bank of England is to manage the national debt. In order to service this as cheaply as possible, low interest rates are desirable. But who will buy the debt if interest rates are lower than the current/expected rate of inflation? The interest rate must be sufficiently attractive to induce investors to buy Government stock. Similarly, an increase in interest rates may be necessary to attract capital inflows from abroad when reserves are falling or there is a deficit balance of payments. Yet a high rate of interest for this purpose will make the cost of domestic borrowing rise, and discourage private sector investment.

One objective has to take priority over another. Low interest rates tend to encourage new investment and increase economic growth. They also help to keep down the cost of Government borrowing. But they may encourage consumption spending on imported goods, or outflows of foreign capital to countries with higher interest rates/stronger currencies.

Change from fiscal to monetary policy

In the United Kingdom during the 1950s and 1960s, fiscal policy was mainly used for demand management. Monetary policy was considered less important. This attitude changed in the 1970s. For a short period after Competition and Credit Control in 1971, the clearing banks were able to expand credit. They had excess liquidity and were now free from direct controls. Exchange rates were allowed to float in 1972 and thus became, in theory, self-adjusting. Monetary policy could now be used for the management of the domestic economy. The large Budget deficits of 1972 and 1973 failed to generate the economic growth hoped for. Instead the money supply increased. This, coupled with the oil price rises, helped to push United Kingdom inflation to new heights. Monetary policy therefore took on a new importance, and there was a swing away from fiscal policy as a method of controlling the economy. More emphasis was placed on the monetary aggregates and, until 1979, prices and incomes policies. In 1981 the authorities began using short-term interest rates as a leverage for monetary control.

'Targets'

In the late 1970s, the main thrust of monetary policy was for control of the money supply by a target or limit on its growth. The reason for publicly declaring quantitative targets from 1976 onwards was summed up by the Governor of the Bank of England (February 1978) as 'the acceleration of inflation'. It was thought that if a specific monetary aggregate were announced as having to be achieved within a certain time span, this would lower inflationary expectations. Further, the monetary aggregate chosen could be adjusted at some intermediate stage if required (a 'rolling' target), thus giving more flexibility.

Money supply control

The authorities (the Treasury and Bank of England) try to control the money supply in two main ways: by (a) market intervention and (b) portfolio constraints. Market intervention relies on the power of the Bank of England as dealer in the financial markets to influence the availability of assets and their rate of return. By using the techniques at its disposal, the Bank can affect the desire of the public to hold money balances, and the willingness of financial institutions to take deposits and to lend. Portfolio constraints restrict certain institutions, mainly banks, from acquiring different kinds of assets and liabilities, so as to prevent an expansion of deposits. The reason for making banks subject to these portfolio restraints is that, unlike other financial institutions, they are able to create bank deposits which form the largest part of the money supply.

Techniques of money supply control

The Government can use specific techniques to affect the money stock and the rate of interest, though the effects are not always precise. There is thought to be a time lag of maybe two years or more between an increase in the money supply and price changes.

(a) *Assets:* The authorities may impose a reserve asset, which banks must keep against their liabilities. If the authorities control the supply of those assets, they can control the banks' creation of deposits.

(b) *Deposits:* The authorities can alter the banks' liabilities instead of their assets. Thus, special deposits were introduced in 1958. Supplementary special deposits (the 'corset'), a still stronger measure, came in 1973 and were not abolished until 1980.

(c) *Directives:* Before Competition and Credit Control, 1971, a favourite money supply control was by directive or guideline. The banks were 'guided' as to the amounts they could lend (quantitative controls) or to whom they could lend, e.g., industrialists, exporters or farmers (qualitative controls). Directives were abandoned in 1971 but the Bank periodically gave advice on suitable/unsuitable cases for loans.

(d) *Financing the public sector borrowing requirement:* Another method of control is in the way the public sector borrowing requirement is financed. When total public spending exceeds total public revenue, there is a public sector borrowing requirement. If the money is financed by United Kingdom residents, there is no increase in the money supply. The Government overspends in one sector or on one group of the domestic economy and recoups the same amount from other groups. The money supply has not increased; it has been redistributed. If the Government finances its borrowing by the sale of stock to foreigners overseas, again there is no increase in the money supply. This will only arise if foreigners buy stock from United Kingdom residents and thereby increase the latters' bank deposits. Money supply increases if the Government borrows from the banks, or prints more notes.

(e) *Interest rates:* Before Competition and Credit Control, the authorities relied on the use of bank rate to influence market rates of interest. After 1971, interest rates became market determined. The philosophy behind the introduction of minimum lending rate and the abolition of bank rate was that there should be no direct controls on the availability of credit. It should be available at a price (interest). But bank rate had to come back because the authorities wished to retain control of interest rates, and to show by movements in bank rate how they wanted market rates to move. As every student of monopoly knows, it is not possible to control both the supply of a commodity and its price. If price is controlled, the market will show by its demand patterns how much of the commodity it wants or can buy at the given price. If supply is controlled, then the price can soar to heights determined by the intensity (elasticity) of demand. Money is not immune from these economic laws. Nevertheless, the authorities often try to manipulate both money supply and interest rates. The monetary control measures of 1981 gave greater strength to the discount market and emphasised short-term interest rate changes as a method of monetary control.

(f) *The Banking Act 1979:* This came into force to harmonise with EEC policies, which had stricter regulation of deposit-taking institutions than the apparently looser system prevailing in the United Kingdom. The Act set up a statutory framework for the establishment of a two-tier system of recognised banks and licensed deposit takers. It introduced a scheme for the protection of deposits, it aimed for greater clarity on banks' existing restraints and the supervision of deposit takers and it aimed for greater financial control. The title 'bank' would be allowed only to authorised operators.

(g) *Monetary control measures 1981:* As a result of the Banking Act, and the large new number of institutions subject to supervision, a new monetary sector was defined for the purposes of monetary control. This covered: (a) recognised banks and licensed deposit takers; (b) the National Girobank; (c) the trustee savings banks; (d) those banks in the Channel Islands and the Isle of Man that decided to join the cash ratio scheme; and (e) the banking department of the Bank of England.

The cash ratio meant that all institutions in the monetary sector with eligible liabilities of £10m or more had to hold ½% of those liabilities as non-earning balances at the Bank of England. *Special deposits*, when called for, applied to the same institutions. *Eligible banks* were introduced so that, providing certain criteria were met, the Bank would discount bills from a far wider range of banks than previously and thus be assured of an adequate supply of bills for its open market operations. These 'eligible banks' had to hold at least 4% of their eligible liabilities with the discount houses each day, and 6% of their deposits with them on an average daily basis over six or twelve months. This constraint was removed in 1983. The average daily liability that banks had to hold with the discount houses was reduced from 6% to 5%. The minimum daily percentage was also reduced from 4% of eligible liabilities to 2.5%. The reason for the change was that the eligible liabilities of banks had grown far faster than had been anticipated. The loss to the discount houses was estimated at £750m. To compensate them for this change they were allowed to carry assets forty times their capital base. This multiplier of 40 depends on the riskiness of assets held. Thus, fixed rate gilts over five years, whose value can fluctuate sharply, count three times in calculating a house's total books, whereas less risky (short-term) gilts count only once. Houses wishing to deal in higher risk stocks will, therefore, have to keep tighter limits.

Questions on monetary policy

Q1. Discuss the view that it is possible to control either the money supply or the level of interest rates, but not both. What practical implications does this view have for the way in which the monetary authorities seek to control the money supply?

A1. The money supply in a country comprises bank deposits and notes and coin in circulation, the latter being important only in very undeveloped economies. Monetary control is therefore levelled on bank deposits. If these increase so does the money supply and vice versa. If the authorities try to use interest rates as a control measure (ignoring the impact on the economy), they come up against the dilemma of any monopolist: price (which in this case is interest) and supply (which in this case is money) cannot be controlled simultaneously. Raising interest rates to reduce the money supply may have the opposite effect to that desired, e.g., encouraging more time deposits or inflows of foreign capital, and in both cases increasing money supply. The demand for money is interest inelastic in the short run, so that trying to regulate interest rates can affect the supply of money in a direction opposite to that required.

Because it is impossible to control interest rates and the supply of money together, the monetary authorities often try different types of controls, using whatever seems most effective for the particular objective in view, e.g., reserve asset ratios or direct curbs on lending by quality or quantity. Such controls prove ineffective when money is hard to get, for borrowers will go outside the banking system, as happened when the 'corset' was in operation.

Since 1981 the Bank of England has adopted control of short-term interest rates as a policy measure. The monetary authorities also set 'targets' in terms of money supply growth. When these are exceeded, other policy measures are adopted, such as aggressive marketing of gilts or direct cuts in public spending, both of which reduce the money supply. Monetary base control would give direct control over the money supply but has been opposed on the grounds that the volatility of interest rates would make it impossible to control money supply and interest rates together.

Q2. Describe the basic techniques by which central banks operate domestic monetary policy, and the relationship they must have with the commercial banks if they are to do so effectively.

A2. The basic techniques by which central banks operate domestic monetary policy are through: (a) changes in the discount rate; (b) the reserve asset ratio, if any; (c) open market operations; and by (d) regulation, direction and moral suasion. For these techniques to be effective, the central bank must be in a position to monopolise note issue, to hold or control some part of the liquid assets of the commercial banks and to vary the level or type of their reserves by interest rate changes or other means. Without this latter power, open market operations by the central bank are unlikely to be effective.

Q3. Outline the Bank of England's 'funding policy' in respect of Government debt, showing why such a policy is needed and how it is carried out.

A3. A funding policy is one which changes short-term into long-term debt. Funding is necessary because when short-dated stock reaches maturity it is redeemed, and so increases the money supply. This increase may conflict with Government targets at that time. The Bank of England therefore enters the market, buying when the market is falling to check the fall, or to take in a maturing stock at a price below par; selling when the market is high and a large parcel of debt will be taken up by the non-bank public. A funding policy pushes forward the date when the bank has to buy back maturing gilts. It avoids large sums entering the market and affecting equity, gilt and other prices. The object of the Bank's funding policy is to smooth out the peaks and troughs of money flows and to ensure that a suitable amount of National Debt is continually held by individuals and institutions.

Q4. To what extent is a successful anti-inflationary policy necessarily associated with an increase in unemployment? Illustrate your answer with reference to the economic experience of any one country.

A4. Anti-inflationary policy usually takes the form of control of the money supply. It is generally believed in the United Kingdom that the velocity of money is fairly stable, and that if the monetary growth is controlled, inflation will come down. The transmission mechanism by which this happens is not fully understood, so that it is impossible to say how long it will take for a tight monetary policy to reduce inflation. The time period depends partly on wage levels and prices which are set in response to the monetary restrictions.

There appears to be a correlation between unemployment and the ratio of earnings to money supply. Thus, in the United Kingdom during the decade from 1970 to 1980, there were two periods when earnings grew faster than money supply and unemployment grew rapidly. The Phillips curve is the best-known theory that attempts to link the 'trade-off' in terms of unemployment with price stability. With a 1% inflation rate in 1963 there would be 5.5% unemployment. In 1968, the comparative figures would be 4% and 3%. During the 1960s the cost of absolute price stability would be an approximate 8% unemployment rate. If workers respond to price increases by higher wage demands, unemployment tends to increase more rapidly.

Anti-inflationary policies, other than monetary restrictions, include import controls to protect home employment, fiscal policies to restrict aggregate demand and prices and income policies to stabilise domestic prices and prevent an escalation of incomes. So far, however, no solution has appeared to the problem of achieving price stability without at the same time increasing the levels of unemployment.

(Note to student: a good commentary on the above problems can be found in *Economic Progress Report*, No. 123, July 1980, 'Monetary Policy and the Economy', and No. 126 'Earnings and Unemployment.')

Q5. One of your large company customers is the subsidiary of an American multinational company and the directors have asked you to give a brief (ten-minute) talk to their colleagues from the United States on the operation of monetary policy in the United Kingdom. Prepare a paper setting out the salient features of United Kingdom domestic monetary policy in the late 1970s, making comparisons where appropriate with monetary policy in the United States.

A5. The salient features of United Kingdom domestic monetary policy in the late 1970s were a change of direction in monetary policy objectives and techniques. At the beginning of the decade, the aims of monetary policy had altered little from those set out in the Radcliffe Report. At the end of the decade, there was one main objective: the control of inflation. To achieve this meant concern with monetary aggregates and control of the money supply. The big change in this decade, therefore, was the switch from fiscal policy as a measure of controlling the economy to monetary policy as a measure of controlling the money supply. After 1976 when publicly declared quantitative targets were first announced, the emphasis grew on controlling the monetary aggregates as a proximate target for policy. Demand management was quite out of favour. To implement this new type of monetary policy, certain techniques had to be used. Interest rates are the main determinants of the demand for money, but what of the supply side? What interest rate will bring demand and supply into equilibrium? More important still, what level of interest rate will bring demand to the point that the authorities would want? The method used until 1981 was a negative one: to look at the components of the money supply and predict what that supply was likely to be, with and without a change in interest rates. In this way the United Kingdom authorities were using methods similar to those used in the United States, Canada and Germany, i.e., to affect monetary growth by varying the general level of interest rates. United Kingdom domestic banks were controlled more loosely than the United States banks before the Banking Act became law, and the reserve asset ratio then favoured in the United Kingdom was not as rigid as the United States cash base ratio which could be altered by the Federal Reserve.

Special deposits, which were retained under the August 1981 measures, siphon off deposits from the banks into a special account at the Bank of England. There is no corresponding control in the United States. The open market operations used by the Bank of England are similar to those used in the States, although the US system is technically meant to relieve the liquidity of the member banks. Since the 1980 United States Deregulation and Monetary Control Act, the system there has much in common with the 1971 Competition and Credit Control measures in the United Kingdom. Both tried to stimulate competition and control credit in the banking system.

In 1983 both countries were using targets; open market operations to affect interest rates and pursuing monetary policies to reduce inflation. Some degree of deflationary success has been achieved but employment levels, in the United Kingdom at least, have spiralled downwards since 1980, introducing problems which may be even more difficult to solve than those associated with inflation.

Topic 7

Fiscal Policy

Definition of fiscal policy. Government revenue and expenditure; the control of surpluses and deficits in the economy, and the National Debt in particular. The aims and various forms of taxation. A comparison of monetary and fiscal policy.

Fiscal policy: definition

Fiscal policy means using the Budget to alter the level of aggregate demand. It incorporates not merely taxation, as many students think, but also Government spending and borrowing. Keynesian theory suggests that there is an optimum level of demand where full employment can be achieved without inflation. The Phillips curve suggests that there is a trade-off between the two: prices rise as full employment is reached. Higher employment levels can only be achieved at the cost of higher prices. Keynesians hold that Budget deficits are necessary weapons against recession and unemployment. The danger is that expansive Government borrowing makes the control of money supply growth more difficult. Such borrowing can also crowd out private sector investment. Fiscal policy is concerned with the Treasury's revenue and expenditure. It affects money stock and money flow, but the policy is aimed at changing aggregate demand. (Monetary policy is concerned with measures affecting the supply of money.) For a comparison of fiscal and monetary policy, *see* pages 56-57.

The Budget: This is the statement presented to Parliament by the Chancellor of the Exchequer to explain how the Government will raise the revenue to cover its expenditure in the forthcoming year.

Government revenue and expenditure

The bulk of Government revenue comes from two main sources and two minor ones. The major ones are the Inland Revenue and Customs and Excise; the minor ones are motor vehicle duties and miscellaneous receipts. The latter include television and radio licences, fines and fees such as those paid for registration of births, marriages and deaths. All Government revenue and expenditure originally went through one account: the Consolidated Fund. In 1968, however, the National Loans Fund was set up to incorporate all items relating to the National Debt. The National Insurance Fund was introduced after the National Insurance Act of 1945 and is also administered separately, to relate receipts more closely to benefits. The Government makes contributions to the Fund. These are budgeted for annually in the supply services. The Fund also receives income from investments controlled by the National Debt Office.

The National Debt

This is the money owed by the Government to various debtors. In the United Kingdom it comprises the total liabilities of the National Loans Fund plus the stock of the nationalised industries guaranteed by the Government. Debt management involves getting enough money for the Government's needs at the lowest possible cost, and smoothing out the flow of funds arising from different maturity dates. Official holders of the Debt include the National Insurance and other funds, held by the National Debt Commissioners for Investment; the Bank of England Issue Department against the note issue; the Banking Department against liabilities; and overseas central banks. Private holders include banks, insurance companies, pension funds and private individuals. The National Debt can be a burden in two sets of circumstances. One is when its servicing results in loss of incentive to work or schemes to avoid the payment of the tax burden. The other situation is when capital is raised abroad. Repayment involves a currency risk and, meanwhile, interest payments have to be serviced. This outflow reduces the earnings on a country's invisibles and may exacerbate difficulties with the balance of payments. *Marketable debt* is saleable in money markets and on the Stock Exchange. *Non-marketable debt* is not. It includes non-transferable assets, such as premium bonds and national savings.

Central Government borrowing requirement

After the revenue and expenses of the Consolidated Fund are totalled, the surplus or deficit is carried over to the National Loans Fund. A deficit creates a borrowing requirement by the Government; a surplus reduces the need to borrow.

The public sector borrowing requirement

This is local authorities' and public corporations' net borrowing from sources other than the Government, added to the Central Government borrowing requirement. This total, the public sector borrowing requirement, is financed by borrowing from the non-bank private sector, the banking sector (which increases the money supply) and from overseas.

Public finance

This deals with the income and expenditure of Central Government, nationalised industries and local authorities. Decisions of public finance alter the value and distribution of the wealth produced in order to obtain, it is hoped, maximum social and economic advantage for the community.

Taxation

The aims of taxation can be summed up in three ways. First is *allocation:* finding enough money for the various needs of the nation. Secondly, there is *stabilisation:* using the spending powers of the Government to increase/decrease total spending (aggregate demand), and thus to influence the levels of output and employment. Thus, a Budget surplus will be aimed for when the Government wants to reduce demand. (The Government takes more in taxes and the public has less money.) A Budget deficit will be aimed for when the Government wants to increase demand. (The Government takes less in taxes and the public has more money.) The third aim of taxation is *redistribution:* which means taking from the richer and giving to the poorer.

These three aims of taxation; allocation, stabilisation and redistribution overlap. For example, services provided by the public sector and local authorities (allocation) reduce inequalities of income (redistribution). The canons or principles of taxation laid down by Adam Smith were economy (of collection), equity (contributions should be related to the ability to pay), certainty (the tax should be calculable, not some arbitrary sum) and finally convenience, e.g., the payment of tax should not be at some point far from the tax payer's home. Other principles can be added to these original ones of Adam Smith's: the disincentive effect, if any, of high taxes and simplicity.

Some tax definitions

'Fiscal drag' is the term given to the 'dragging' of low income earners (usually because of inflation) into the Revenue's net. 'Fiscal boost', by contrast, reduces the value of fixed sums paid as tax. *Proportionate taxation* is a method of taxation whereby the same proportion of income is paid in taxes, irrespective of the size of income, so that at a 10% tax rate, the £10,000 a year income earner pays £100 in tax, and the £20,000 earner pays £200. *Progressive taxation* ensures that a higher proportion of tax is paid as income increases and vice versa. *Regressive taxation* is where a smaller proportion of tax is paid as income increases. *Indirect taxation* is a system whereby tax goes to the Government indirectly. Its *impact* or *burden* falls upon one person, but its *incidence* (where the burden ultimately falls) can be shifted to another. If a taxed good has an elastic demand, the shopkeeper might himself pay the tax to reduce the price for the buyer, in which case the impact and incidence fall on the same person – the shopkeeper. With an inelastic demand for a good, the tax will be paid by the buyer. The impact is still on the shopkeeper, but the incidence (or burden of actually paying it) has shifted from seller to buyer. Examples of direct tax are income tax, capital gains tax and corporation tax. Capital transfer tax appears to be a direct tax, but payment is often shifted to heirs. Examples of indirect tax are customs and excise duties and VAT.

Table 4: Contrasts between monetary and fiscal policy

Monetary policy	Fiscal policy
Flexible in timing (can be introduced at any time).	Changes are difficult to introduce except in the annual Budget (although the Regulator can be used for certain taxes).
Pervasive.	Specific.

Impact difficult to assess in advance.	Impact can be fairly accurately assessed and quantified.
Public sector investment is restricted by neither the cost of borrowing nor the availability of credit, so the effect is felt most heavily by the private sector (crowding out effect).	Effect is general through overall demand. Public sector is included. Can be highly selective in terms of individuals, industries and regions.
Quick to introduce, slow to take effect.	Takes effect very quickly; new taxes can be applied almost immediately although they need ultimate sanction from Parliament.

Questions on fiscal policy

Questions on fiscal policy, like those on monetary policy, require in answer knowledge of the different policy measures and their aims and effect upon the economy, particularly on the banking sector. Sometimes the candidate is asked to compare/contrast the advantages/disadvantages of monetary and fiscal policies, or to assess their relative effectiveness in pursuing different policy aims.

Q1. Fiscal policy has been likened to heavy artillery in that it is 'slow to move and indiscriminate in its effect'. Discuss this view and consider to what extent fiscal policy has achieved its aims in any one country in recent years.

A1. Fiscal policy means the use of changes in public expenditure and revenue to achieve a surplus or deficit of funds in order to achieve an economic final objective. Such objectives in the past have been stable prices, full employment, economic growth and equilibrium in the balance of payments. In the United Kingdom these objectives have not been achieved simultaneously, either by the use of monetary of fiscal policy or by a mixture of these policies and others. Changes in public revenue and expenditure arise partly from changes in taxation. Such tax changes must generally have approval of Parliament (although the 'Regulator' allows some exceptions to this general rule) and cannot therefore be introduced as an immediate measure. Time may also elapse before changes in direct taxation come into effect. Similarly, changes in public expenditure take time to implement when large projects are involved. Once started they cannot be stopped half-way (half a bridge is no good to anyone). Interest rates (with monetary policy) can be changed overnight with an immediate effect on bond prices.

Fiscal policy is more specific than monetary policy. Tax changes, including benefits, have definite targets: people, industries, regions, goods. (Note, however, that in the public sector, investment grants, subsidies, etc., can also benefit specific groups.) Interest rate changes affect everybody, directly or indirectly, and the same disadvantage arises with a target on money supply growth. It can be seen, then, that in general fiscal policy is indeed 'slow to move and indiscriminate in its effect'.

Q2. 'Keynesians are fiscalists.' Explain this statement. To what extent is it true?

A2. In *General Theory of Employment, Interest and Money*, Keynes says that: 'The outstanding faults . . . of the economic society in which we live are its failure to provide for full employment and its arbitrary and inequitable distribution of wealth and incomes.' To achieve as near a state of full employment as possible, Keynes recommended changes in aggregate demand. The main weapon for changing aggregate demand was the Budget. If demand was too low, Government spending should be increased; if demand was too high, Government spending should be reduced or taxation increased. Keynes and his followers can therefore be said to be 'fiscalists', for they regarded the Budget as the main instrument of aggregate demand. Monetary policy was, in their view, only an adjunct to fiscal policy.

When fiscal policy appeared ineffective in controlling inflation, many Keynesians suggested import controls or incomes policies as methods of influencing the economy and increasing employment without raising prices. But Keynesians remain basically 'fiscalists', in that they regard changes in Government spending and revenue as the main way of influencing the economy and the level of employment.

Q3. Outline the various considerations which influence the content of a Government's Budget.

A3. Pre-Keynesian Budgets were almost entirely concerned with devising ways of raising revenue to meet expenditure. Thereafter, wider considerations prevailed. Modern Budgets are more concerned with altering the overall level of demand, though some thought may be given to other factors, e.g., different types or methods of taxation such as negative income tax. The balance of payments situation may require taxes on particular imports. Is income/wealth to be redistributed? If so, how? These are typical questions a Government looks at when considering the content of a present-day Budget.

Q4. Discuss the view that fiscal policy is now too cumbersome an instrument of economic policy because taxes, borrowing and public expenditure form too large a proportion of national income. To what extent can a Government use other types of economic policy to support fiscal policy?

A4. Public expenditure is defined (Cmd 7049) as (a) the current and capital expenditure of Central Government and local authorities (excluding expenditure charged to the operating account of trading bodies); (b) Government finance in the form of grants, loans or public dividend capital provided towards the cost of capital equipment by the nationalised industries and some other public corporations; (c) the capital expenditure of the remaining public corporations; (d) the contingency reserve; and (e) debt interest. In the late 1970s public expenditure was around 45% of Gross Domestic Product, and rose thereafter by about 20%. It is not easy to cut back a large percentage of GDP without a great deal of unemployment in the labour-intensive public sector. High unemployment is expensive in terms of lost productivity, social benefits and social unrest. Income tax can be a rigid instrument of fiscal policy because of the work and delay involved in changing rates (although computerisation is helping here and VAT is quick acting). Fiscal policy is temporarily out of favour, but can be supported by monetary measures, e.g., interest rates, control of the money supply and quantitative or qualitative controls on credit and moral suasion and marketing techniques, such as advertisements to 'Buy British'.

Q5.(a) Distinguish between direct and indirect taxation.

(b) With particular reference to the United Kingdom tax system in the last ten years, examine the arguments for and against a shift from direct to indirect taxation.

A5.(a) The main difference between direct and indirect taxation is that the impact and incidence of the tax fall directly on the same person and cannot be passed on. The impact of indirect taxation can be shifted, depending on the elasticity of demand for the service or good. With an inelastic demand, the buyer will bear the full brunt of the tax; with an elastic demand, the seller will pay at least part of the tax, for the demand will vary with the price of the good or service.

(b) High direct taxation is thought to be a disincentive to output, and, when the starting point is low, very regressive. (The 1978 Rooker Wise clause gave some amelioration here, by linking personal allowances against tax to the retail price index.) An argument for indirect against direct taxation is consumer choice. The less the tax taken from incomes, the more an earner can spend on goods and services. To avoid hardship to the poor, however, indirect taxes should not be levied on basic needs.

Topic 8

The UK Financial System

(a) The nature of financial intermediation. The history, structure, functions, operation and profitability of commercial banks. The relationship of commercial banks to other types of bank and financial institutions.

(b) The functions and methods of operation of the Bank of England.

(c) The money markets, including the discount markets and the various sterling and currency 'wholesale' or 'parallel' markets in London.

This section of the AIB syllabus is perhaps the easiest for students already working in banks. It is, however, very comprehensive, covering the central bank, commercial banks, and other financial institutions as well as the money markets.

Financial intermediation

This is the process by which money is taken from one group, and lent, usually in less liquid form, to another. The institutions involved in financial intermediation are those which offer (a) a means of settling debts; (b) security, interest, convenience and/ or capital appreciation in various degrees for money lodged with them; and (c) contractual savings schemes and protection against specific risks. The first group are mainly banks; the second includes building societies, finance houses, unit and investment trusts and some banks. The third group comprises insurance companies and pension funds.

Banks borrow from one group and lend to others for rather longer terms and therefore in less liquid form. Building societies, finance houses and insurance companies take deposits and lend against mortgages, consumer durables and insurance policies respectively. Unit and investment trusts take deposits for participation in shares. All these institutions are involved in the process of intermediation. The difference between bank and non-bank financial intermediaries is that the liabilities of banks can be used as a medium of exchange; the liabilities of non-bank intermediaries usually cannot be. It should be noted, however, that building societies are gradually taking over some of the functions thought of at one time as bank prerogatives, and their deposits are included in the money supply definition PSL2.

Commercial bank development before 1981

Until the Banking Act was passed in 1979, there was no definition of a bank other than of an institution that carried on the business of banking. Even the 1979 Banking Act did not define a bank, but by creating a three-tier system it categorised banks and financial institutions into a more recognisable structure of banks, licensed deposit takers and other financial institutions. Before 1979, banks could be classified by the current legislation of the time. These were as follows: (a) The '127' banks, so called because under Section 127 of the Companies Act 1963 they were exempt from certain disclosure conditions, and could advertise for deposits. These were the most prestigious banks, such as the clearers. 'Statistical' banks, which periodically provided the Bank of England with statistical information, formed a part of the general group of '127' banks. (b) Banks of a lesser status, known as '123' banks because, under Section 123 of the Companies Act 1967, they were exempt from the provision of the Money Lenders Acts 1900–27. This exemption enabled them to reclaim loans even if they were not licensed money lenders or if they were not classified as banks under previous definitions. A large number of banks crept in under this 'umbrella', obtaining the necessary exemption certificates. (c) 'Authorised' banks, about which there was nothing special except that under the Exchange Control Act 1947, they were authorised to deal in foreign currency and perform certain other delegated functions. Partly as a result of this very wide category of 'banks' ranging from the most prestigious to the less so, partly because of the fringe banking crisis of 1973–4 and partly because of the need for harmonisation of banking law in the EEC, the whole system of bank classi-fication was tidied up by the Banking Act 1979. This Act increased the number of institutions under the supervision of the Bank, and so the new monetary sector was introduced, with its five subdivisions of banks and deposit takers.

Banks need not be classified by the legislation under which they operate, however, but by their function. They may be retail banks in a high street, accepting deposits and providing services such as the safe custody of valuables, executor and trustee business, interspersed with some foreign exchange dealing. Merchant bankers are the wholesalers of banking, providing acceptance credit, raising new issues and giving advice on mergers and take-overs. They operate in the international and Eurocurrency market where many financial institutions, inclu-ding banks, compete for the business available.

Commercial banks

The commercial banks are part of the monetary sector. The direct effect on the commercial banks of an increase in the money stock is that banks increase their lending. This should mean an increase in their profits (if operating costs and interest rates remain constant). In the wholesale markets, the differentials between lending and borrowing will become narrower, so that unless volume improves, profitability could fall. The reverse is true when a decrease in money stock growth takes place. Changes in the country's money stock will influence the economy and, indirectly, the banks. An increase in the stock is likely to mean increase in economic activity and thus more use of the banks' services. If inflation is present or increasing, more loans might be wanted by companies in difficulties, and banks would need to be discriminate in their lending. If the govern-ment is concerned to bring inflation down by monetary means, credit would be restricted and interest rates allowed to rise steeply. The profitability of the banks in this situation will depend on the size of their balance sheets. Operating costs are likely to rise: workers in banks and associated institutions are not immune from rises in living costs. Moreover, they are likely to press for wage claims, particularly if banks are showing good profit figures. If profits are particularly good during periods of high interest there is always the chance that the Government will impose a 'windfall' tax on at least some part of those profits.

The Bank of England

The Bank of England acts in consort with the Treasury. The two are often referred to as the 'monetary authorities'. The Treasury is responsible for overall economic management and the object-ives of monetary policy (such as the level of money stock growth). The Bank acts as the Treasury's agent in carrying out those objectives, using such techniques as the Treasury may determine. In practice, the expertise of the Bank helps to formulate the details of monetary control, and the Bank has wide discretion in its daily money market operations. In addition to its monetary policy role, the Bank's other functions can be summed up as follows: it acts as the Government's banker; as banker for the other banks and discount houses and as lender of last resort to them; as manager of the Exchange Equalisation Account and as a representative of the Government in inter-national monetary institutions such as the IMF, the IBRD, the IDA and the IFC.

In its banking role, the Bank of England is the bank used, for historical reasons, by a small number of private customers as well as by its own staff. It is banker to the clearing banks and to the discount houses. The former use the Bank to settle their indebtedness to one another; the latter need the Bank's last resort facilities. Other banks, too, are customers of the Bank as are overseas central banks and monetary institutions. The Bank also acts as banker to the Government. All the surpluses and debits of individual Government departments go through the Bank. The Bank provides loans and overdrafts to the Government and manages the Government debt. It also issues notes on behalf of the Government, and remits the not inconsiderable profit on this operation to the Treasury. The Bank also has a monetary policy function. It buys and sells securities; it administers any controls on behalf of the Treasury and it uses moral suasion when neces-sary to persuade monetary institutions to accept policies deemed to be the right ones. The Bank also undertakes research and analysis, in order to advise Governments on policy techniques or changes. Finally, the Bank has a regulatory or supervisory function. The Governor represents the views of the City to the Government and vice versa; he has a responsibility for ensuring the good functioning of the City institutions and specifically those of the banking system. Until 1979 all these functions were exercised in an informal way, although the Panel on City Codes and Practices had its Secretariat paid for by the Bank.

In 1979, the Banking Act put many of these functions into a more legislative framework. There were two reasons for abandoning formal and substituting legal controls. One was EEC harmonisation: the need for United Kingdom institutions to have parity with those in the EEC. The other reason for legal controls was the secondary banking crisis of 1973–5 and resulting concern. The number of banks had grown. So, too, had deposits; to such an extent that the adequacy of shareholders' funds was being called into question. When the banking crisis occurred in 1973, a 'lifeboat' operation was put into effect by the clearing banks. Greater supervision was introduced in 1974. In September 1975, the Bank of England published a paper outlining its plans for greater supervision of the banking system, with various aspects of capital adequacy and liquidity to be monitored. A White Paper followed in 1976, presaging the clearer definition of banks and other institutions which was to be set out in the Banking Act of 1979. As a result of this Act with its dual classification of banks and licensed deposit takers, a far greater number of financial institutions came under the Bank of England's supervision. The monetary control measures of 1981 defined the 'monetary sector' as covering all those institutions that came under the new measures of monetary control.

Thus, it could be said that from the banking crisis of 1973 until the Banking Act of 1979, the regulatory function of the Bank of England was strengthened. Thereafter, this function was partly superseded by legislation, but the power of the Bank to accept institutions as 'banks' rather than 'licensed deposit takers' still gives it a very important regulatory role. Its supervisory function over the monetary sector has increased; but lessened in regard to other City institutions. As a bankers' bank it is perhaps more important, for now there are many more banks that have to keep balances at the Bank than previously. As an agent of the Government's monetary policy its role may have weakened; the Banking Act formalised the arrangement by which the Bank acted as agent for the Treasury. Thus, appeals can be made to the Treasury or questions asked in Parliament about the Bank's actions.

The money markets

These include the discount or classical market and the parallel market. The former includes the Bank of England as lender of last resort, the banks and the discount houses. It deals in Treasury bills, local authority and bank bills, short gilts and sterling certificates of deposit. The parallel market comprises three major markets and two minor ones, all part of a unitary unsecured sterling money market in which interest rates differ according to the borrower and instruments being traded. The major markets deal in certificates of deposit, inter-bank and local authority paper; the minor markets include the finance and inter-company markets. On the foreign exchange and currency deposit markets, the most important negotiable instrument is the dollar certificate of deposit.

Market interest rates and yields

Domestic interest rates are affected by liquidity preference, the current marginal return on capital and future expectations, monetary policy and the level of interest rates abroad. Interest rates in the money market reflect more directly the characteristics of different financial claims. (*See also* Topic 5 on Interest Rates.)

Questions on the UK financial system

Questions are not often asked on financial institutions other than the United Kingdom banks. (The United States banking system was dropped from the syllabus some years ago.) But increased competition with banks from building societies, now included in the monetary aggregate PSL2, means that the student must keep a watchful eye on such non-bank financial intermediaries as well as on the monetary sector for any new developments. When answering questions not specific to the United Kingdom, it is also useful to be able to illustrate points with examples from another banking system known to you. The techniques of monetary policy differ at different periods and the student must know those in force at the time of the examination.

A. Financial intermediation and commercial banks

Questions on banks usually ask about their liquidity and profitability. More of the former means less of the latter, and vice versa. But the degree of liquidity a bank holds may be subject to supervision, regulations or guide lines at any given time. Questions on financial institutions other than the banks appear rarely, if at all. Banking students should survey them, however, if only to realise the very stiff competition for deposits that now exists among the financial institutions. An eye should be kept on the monetary sector for any new developments.

Q1. What effects do changes in a country's money stock have on its commercial banks?

A1. An increase in money stock has both direct effects on commercial banks (increased bank lending and usually higher profits) and indirect effects (probable expansion of the economy or inflation, or a combination of the two). In the former case, bank profits will increase because of more consumer/capital spending and increased opportunities for lending. Higher inflation will induce Government action to reduce the growth of the money stock, causing higher interest rates. Bank profits will then depend on the banks' ability to keep to their previous level of lending while holding down operating costs, and to ensure adequate provision for bad debts.

Q2. For what reasons does a commercial bank need liquidity and how may it be provided? How has Bank of England supervision altered since 1981?

A2. A commercial bank needs liquidity: (a) for settlement at the clearing and for withdrawals of deposits; (b) against cash problems arising from commitments already made; and (c) to ensure confidence in the bank. Provision of liquidity comes from: (a) the balances (additional to the ½% cash ratio), which the banks retain at the Bank of England for clearing inter-bank indebtedness; (b) the cash flow generated by maturing assets; (c) a different 'mix' of deposits; and (d) keeping some assets in fairly liquid form. After 1981 there was no requirement for banks to have a minimum reserve asset ratio. The call money ratio of 4–6% which banks had to keep with the discount houses was designed to ensure the continuance of the houses' bill broking activities, rather than as a liquidity measure for the banks. The Bank of England therefore brought out a consultative paper in 1981, which emphasised a cash flow approach to liquidity. Guide-lines showed how this could be achieved and the Bank has tried to ensure that all banks adopt prudent policies with regard to their individual commitments.

Q3. What is meant by liquidity and why does a commercial bank need it? How and to what extent does a commercial bank provide for liquidity in the use of deposits lodged with it?

A3. Liquidity means any type of financial asset which is immediately spendable for its nominal value. Cash is the most liquid of all assets. Thereafter come a range of assets which are increasingly less liquid until we reach those like machinery, fixtures and plant which may be very difficult if not impossible to change into cash at the time required without capital loss. A commercial bank needs liquidity for transactions, precaution and investment. They must retain enough cash to repay customers' money on demand and not allow their balances to fall below a liquidity level that is prudent. The banks may make losses on their investments. Companies to whom they have lent money may go into liquidation and the banks must keep some liquid assets to cover these bad debts.

From the deposits a commercial bank receives, ½% must go to the Bank of England as a cash ratio and about another ½–1% for settling inter-bank indebtedness. A further 5% will go in secured money to the discount houses. The rest can be apportioned in any way the banks see fit. Some will be held in investments which provide income; some in investments with a cash flow by way of different maturities. More liquidity can be arranged by matching wholesale deposits with loans of the same time span and by ensuring with other banks that lines of credit are available in case of need. However, the more liquid the bank becomes, the less profitable it is likely to grow.

Q4. How are the commercial banks in a country affected by the fiscal policy of that country?

A4. Fiscal policy is the method of increasing or decreasing the Government's spending to achieve certain economic ends. If reflation is wanted, the Government will spend more; if deflation is wanted, the Government will spend less. The idea is to increase or decrease aggregate demand in the economy. If the Government increases its spending, recipients of the extra money will either spend or save it. In either case, the money will end up as deposits in banks. The banks' liquidity and reserves will rise. They will be able to increase their advances, and usually their profits. The reverse would be true if the Government tried to spend less. Liquidity and reserves would fall, though not necessarily bank profits. These depend on the difference between rates received from assets and liabilities, minus the costs of running the bank. The larger the size of the balance sheet, the larger will be the profit differential between total assets and total liabilities. A large volume compensates for a small differential. A small volume will have to be compensated for by a larger differential between rates on assets and rates on liabilities. Increased wages or other costs will lower the overall profit. Thus, when interest charges are high, banks are liable to do better because the rates on loans go higher, whereas rates on some part of the liabilities, namely current accounts, remain fixed. Conversely, low interest rates will mean less profit unless costs fall or volume expands. It is generally thought that borrowing will fall when interest rates are high, but companies may have to borrow at high rates as a temporary measure against impending losses. The high rates current in 1980 did not deter many companies from borrowing in that year, as the money supply figures showed.

If the Government tries to finance a deficit through the public rather than through the banks, deposits are likely to fall as customers withdraw their money to buy gilts. Thus, the actual way a deficit is financed has an effect on the overall profitability and liquidity of the banks, as well as the size of the deficit itself. Finally, certain banks will be affected in specific ways. If fiscal policy involves some regional aid or abatement of tax in particular localities, banks in those areas will naturally be affected by that policy in the form of increased economic and banking activity.

Q5. Describe the basic techniques with which central banks operate domestic monetary policy, and the relationship in which they must stand to the commercial banks if they are to do so effectively.
(Note to student: the techniques of monetary policy differ at different times and the student must know those in force at the time of the examination. Note also that the question is not asking for the techniques used only by the Bank of England but those used by central banks generally.)

A5. Central banks use similar basic techniques to influence domestic monetary policy, with variations to suit their own situations. In the United States, for example, reserve requirements are more forceful than in Britain, with different reserve ratios for different classes of banks, depending on their location and balance sheets. Open market operations are used by central banks in most countries, sometimes, as in the United Kingdom, to aid Government debt management. In countries with a smaller National Debt, open market operations are used more as a method of influencing interest rates and credit control. Since 1981 this has also been tried in the United Kingdom, with open market operations used to affect the money supply.

In order for the central banks' techniques to be effective on domestic monetary policy, those techniques must directly or indirectly control the level of the banks' reserves, and thus their ability to lend. This means that the central bank must be: (a) the bankers' bank, so that at least some reserves are under the central bank's direct supervision – a monetary base system gives the strongest control of all; (b) the sole issuer of notes so that one part of the money supply (though the smallest) is under its direct control; and (c) able to control the type and amount of reserves that banks must hold. If it is not all these, the central banks' open market operations would prove ineffective, and legislation would have to be introduced to the effect that required reserves could be obtained only from the central banks.

Q6. Explain briefly the meaning of (a) 'eligible liabilities' and (b) eligible bank bills.

A6. (a) The term 'eligible liabilities' occurred in the Competition and Credit Control document issued in 1971, and was defined in *Reserve Ratios and Special Deposits*, also issued in 1971. They are: (i) sterling deposits with an original maturity of two years or less from United Kingdom residents (excluding banks) and from overseas residents; funds temporarily held in suspense accounts (that is, amounts due to customers and third parties); (ii) sterling inter-bank deposits and sterling certificates of deposits on a net basis, including a bank's net deposit liability in sterling to its overseas offices; (iii) a bank's net liabilities in currencies other than sterling; and (iv) 60% of the net value of items in transit. In 1981, all institutions in the monetary sector with eligible liabilities of £10m or more had to keep ½% of such liabilities in non-interest earning balances at the Bank of England. In the calculation of eligible liabilities offsets were allowed in respect of funds lent to other institutions in the monetary sector, and money placed at call with money brokers and gilt-edged jobbers on the Stock Exchange; secured on gilt-edged stocks, Treasury bills, local authority bills and bills accepted by 'eligible' banks.

(b) Eligible bank bills are those which are eligible for re-discount at the Bank of England. Before the monetary control measures of 1981 these bank bills comprised only those accepted by the London and Scottish clearing banks, the members of the

Accepting Houses Committee and the major British Overseas and Commonwealth banks. After the monetary control measures, the number of such 'eligible banks' increased. The criteria used by the Bank for judging eligible status (that is, those banks whose bills would be acceptable for re-discount) were whether: (i) the applicant had a broadly based and substantial acceptance business in the United Kingdom; (ii) its acceptances commanded the finest rates in the market for ineligible bills; and (iii) if the bank were foreign owned, British banks enjoyed reciprocal opportunities in the foreign owners' domestic markets. The mere possession of these criteria did not automatically ensure eligible status to any bank, but by August 1981 over 90 banks had been granted eligibility.

Q7. What were the reasons for the Banking Act of 1979 and what were the results?

A7. The Banking Act resulted from (a) the fringe banking crisis, which led to doubts about the prudential regulation of the banking system on a non-statutory basis, and (b) the regulatory requirements of the EEC regarding financial institutions under the EEC Council Directive of December 1977. The Banking Act 1979 followed the White Paper. It set up a three-tier structure of banks, licensed deposit takers and other financial institutions such as building societies and Friendly Societies who operate under other legislation. Only recognised banks may use the word 'bank' in their title. To be 'recognised', a bank must have had a good reputation in the financial community; current and deposit accounts in sterling and foreign currency; loan and overdraft facilities; a wide range of banking services and one of the following three: foreign exchange services, bill finance or advice on dealing in sterling or foreign currencies. The 'wide range of banking services' had to include five service components: deposit facilities in sterling or foreign currencies; foreign exchange and fund transmission facilities; trade finance facilities and financial or investment advisory services. The Bank could waive all five requirements of the 'wide range of banking services' if an applicant provided a 'highly specialised banking service' necessary to the banking sector. This applicant had to be able to provide deposit facilities in sterling or foreign currencies; loan facilities in sterling or foreign currencies and one of the three other types of service.

Any institutions that did not meet these provisions were

classified as 'licensed deposit takers'. To be in this category, the finance house or other institution had to show that it had adequate liquidity to provide against bad and doubtful debts, and sufficient net assets to safeguard depositors, with reference to its balance of assets and liabilities. Insurance cover had to be provided for depositors against loss. If a deposit taker's licence was granted, the institution would have two years to cast out any reference to 'bank' in its title. If the institution applying for a deposit taker's licence does not satisfy the requirements of the Bank of England's banking supervision department, it may get only a twelve-month provisional licence. An appeal may be made to the Chancellor of the Exchequer but few deposit-taking institutions are in practice likely to do so. On any point of law, they may appeal to the High Court. This again is an unlikely development. Since the Act became law, five leading finance houses, all previously classed as banks, were recognised only as licensed deposit-taking institutions. The same fate befell five previously listed banks, i.e., statistical banks for reporting purposes. The Act provided for re-grading at the Bank of England's discretion.

Q8.(a) Using the figures shown in Table 5 as a guide, assess the role of the United Kingdom banks in channelling finance for trade and industry.
(b) What other figures are needed in order to prepare a complete assessment of the adequacy of bank finance for trade and industry?

Table 5: United Kingdom banking sector (sterling) 31 March 1979

	Deposits from UK residents	Lending to UK residents (including holdings of securities issued by public and private sectors)
	£m	£m
Public sector		
Central government	518	6,128
Local authorities	241	4,881
Public corporations	383	600
Private sector		
Industrial and commercial companies	11,133	24,169
Personal sector	24,901	11,259

Other financial institutions	5,357	3,534
	42,533	50,571

Note: The discrepancy between the two columns is due to the omission of non-deposit liabilities, such as capital and reserves, and the omission of data relating to overseas residents.

A8.(a) The figures in Table 5 show that the banks play an important role in channelling finance for trade and industry. Deposits from the private sector (£24,901m) almost match the amount (£24,169m) lent by the banks to industrial and commercial companies. By contrast, the private sector received only £11,259m as loans. The banks are acting as intermediaries: channelling funds between sectors and converting short-term deposits into longer advances. While the total received from the public sector in the form of deposits was £1,142m (518 + 241 + 383m), the public sector received £11,609 (6,128 + 4,881 + 600m) in the form of loans. If the public sector spent these loans on capital goods, money would thereby be channelled into trade and industry. On the other hand, lending by the banks to the public sector could 'crowd out' direct demands from trade and industry for funds. The Wilson Committee, set up in 1977 to consider the provision of funds for trade and industry, reported on small firms' difficulty in raising finance and of bigger firms in getting long-term loans. Since the report, the Government has taken a hand in providing finance for small firms with 'start up' and other schemes.

(b) Further figures needed to prepare a complete assessment of the adequacy of bank finance for trade and industry are: (i) A breakdown of the internal and external sources of funds available to companies. It would then be possible to compare the percentage of internal funds (retained profits, trade credit) with external funds, such as bank overdrafts, new issues of equity or loan capital and/or Government subsidies. (ii) It would also be useful to know the total demand for capital from the banks. Without this knowledge, nobody can tell whether the amount which banks lend to trade and industry is sufficient or by how much it falls short. (iii) It might also be useful to learn, when funds were refused, the reason why.

Q9. Describe the role and assess the significance of building societies.

(Note to student: although the Institute of Bankers' syllabus covers the relationship of commercial banks to other types of bank and financial institution, questions on non-bank financial intermediaries have occasionally been asked.)

A9. There are over 300 building societies and some 80% are members of the Building Societies Association. Their role is twofold: to provide (a) relatively cheap finance for home owner-ship and (b) a safe depositary for small savings. The societies take in over £30bn of deposits and attract about 40% of savings; both figures of which are rapidly increasing with some aggres-sive marketing. The significance of the building societies is that, as non-bank financial intermediaries, they channel savings to the housing market and hence the construction industry. It is often urged by the banks that the societies have unfair advan-tages: they have an arrangement with the Inland Revenue by which depositors are paid net of basic rate tax; they did not have to keep within the confines of the 'corset' when it was in oper-ation, nor do they have to hold any part of their deposits as balances at the Bank of England. On the other hand, banks paid interest gross until 1984, which was an advantage to the small saver who did not pay tax. Further, by supplying long-term capital, the building societies release bank deposits for shorter-term investment. In 1980, the banks started moving into the home loan market with lending rates for potential home buyers that were sometimes more competitive than those offered to young entrepreneurs trying to set up first-time businesses. As the recession developed, banks moved away from home loans into their more traditional shorter-term lending. Building society deposits (excluding term shares and the SAYE arrange-ments) minus their holdings of money market instruments and bank deposits, etc., are now included in the money supply aggregate PSL2.

Q10. Describe the role and assess the significance of the National Girobank.

A10. The National Giro was set up in 1968 as a sector of the Post Office Corporation. The Post Office Act 1969 and the Post Office (Banking Services) Act 1976 gave the Giro wider powers. It no longer operated only as a current account and money banking transmission service with a computerised head office at Bootle, Lancashire. The 1976 legislation allowed for the development of general banking services, including overdrafts; and in 1978, deposit accounts were introduced. A limited amount of cash can be obtained at many of the 21,000 post offices which are part of the Girobank. In 1981, the Girobank became part of the monetary sector and subject to its provisions.

B. The Bank of England

Q11. Compare and contrast the techniques used by the Bank of England in implementing monetary policy with those used by the central bank of another country with which you are familiar. (Note to student: before answering this question it should be remembered that fiscal policy is concerned with the Treasury's revenue and expenditure. It affects money stock and money flow but the policy is aimed at changing aggregate demand. *Monetary policy* is concerned with measures affecting *the supply of money*. The other point to remember is that when presented with this type of question, and the similar 'for/against' or 'advantages/disadvantages' type, do not simply list the similarities or dissimilarities involved. The best way of tackling these questions is to learn the facts by means of a written list to help recall, but when answering the exam question, balance each 'for' (advantage, etc.) with its corresponding 'against' (disadvantage, etc.). Provide a conclusion or emphasise a theme. The main themes in *this* question are the techniques of monetary policy, with examples from two different central banks.)

A11. The techniques used by the United States Federal Reserve to implement monetary policy are similar to those used by the Bank of England before 1981. They are reserve requirements, open market operations, the Federal Funds discount rate (the equivalent of bank rate) and moral suasion. The Bank of England carries out the monetary policy of the United Kingdom Government as an agent of the Treasury. In the United States, monetary policy and its implementation are directed by the Board of Governors, who are appointed by the President. The Open Market Committee decide policy on open market operations, with the president of the New York Bank always being a member of the committee. In the United Kingdom, the Bank of England carries out open market operations to smooth the flow of funds in the banking system and to affect the level of interest rates. The two functions of affecting bank credit (and thus the money stock) and of stabilising the market are separated in the United States. Straight sales and purchases of stock affect commercial bank deposits, while arrangements with a dealer for the sale and repurchase of stock (similar to London Stock Exchange contangos) offset any destabilising flow of funds. United States reserve requirements, after the 1980 Monetary Control Act, extended to non-member banks. These requirements distinguished between time and demand deposits and the size and location of banks. The assets had to be in bank cash and in deposits with the Federal Reserve. In Britain the reserve ratio was not a legal requirement and it could be kept in a variety of forms, including deposits at the Bank.

The liquidity supervision of the Bank of England, operative in Britain since the Monetary Control measures of 1981, is not mandatory as it is in the United States system. It relies on guidelines to establish prudent policies for individual banks. Interest rates are used in both countries as a technique of control. In the United Kingdom the idea is to influence the short-term money market. In the United States this policy operated in the decade between 1952–62 but was found to give too little leverage on the structure of interest rates. The Federal Open Market Committee now operates on Government securities of all maturities.

Q12. What is meant by 'the note circulation'?

A12. The note circulation is the issue of notes by the Bank of England to the high street banks who use the notes in the course of their business. The Bank debits the banks' accounts when the notes are handed over, and invests the money thus received. The business is highly profitable. On a note issue of around £1,300m, all but £30m (expenses for producing, handling and storing the notes) is profit. But because the Bank of England has to hold Government securities among its other assets as 'collateral' for the notes, almost all the profit goes to the Treasury. The Bank of England takes its share of expenses, plus interest on the Government securities held as backing for the note issue. The Government, through the Bank of England and the Treasury, got from the note circulation in 1980 interest-free credit of around £10,000m.

Q13. Outline the major commercial factors which influence the distribution and growth of a commercial bank's assets. In what ways has the Bank of England influenced the structure of bank balance sheets in the United Kingdom from 1972 to 1982?

(Note to student: this is typical of questions that appear about once a year on bank liquidity and profitability.)

A13. The growth of a commercial bank's assets depends on the growth and type of deposits. Large and long-term deposits give greater opportunities for increasing the banks' asset structure. So, too, does an increase in lending, but this has to be balanced against the risks involved, and considerations of capital adequacy. Distribution of a bank's assets is affected by the need for liquidity and any regulations regarding reserves or other ratios that must be observed.

The Bank of England has influenced the structure of banks' balance sheets in the 10 years to 1982 in the following ways: (a) By ratios that had to be observed, beginning with the 12.5% reserve asset ratio of Competition and Credit Control in 1971. (b) The supplementary special deposit scheme ('the corset') was designed to restrict the growth of interest-bearing deposits. (c) The cash ratio of ½% was lodged with the Bank of England after the 1981 measures; and a further 4–6% of liabilities with the discount houses. (d) Aggressive selling of public sector debt by the Bank of England financed the Government's borrowing requirement. (This has meant that the banks hold a lower proportion of their assets in such debt.) (e) Raising of interest rates sometimes, though not always, slows down the level of bank advances. (f) Rules regarding the levels of capital adequacy and liquidity issued since the Banking Act 1979 have also altered the distribution of banks' assets.

Q14. How do central banks act as 'lenders of last resort'?

A14. Central banks act as 'lenders of last resort' by lending to commercial banks when those banks are temporarily short of required funds. In the United Kingdom the Bank of England lends almost invariably via the discount houses to the banks. The banks then recall the money they have lent to the discount houses. Central bank lending may be at a penal rate but much depends on the monetary policy being pursued at the time. During the era of fixed exchange rates, and at other times of credit restriction, the Bank of England provided last resort lending at penal rates. This is often not the case in the United States, where last resort lending is invariably used to improve liquidity and not to influence reserves. The Federal Reserve's last resort lending is supposed to enable banks to meet:

'a sudden withdrawal of deposits or seasonal requirements for

credit beyond those which can reasonably be met by its own resources . . . or . . . for longer periods when necessary, in order to assist member banks in meeting unusual situations such as may result from national, regional or local difficulties.'
(Regulation A)

However, continuous recourse to the Discount Window (through which the Federal Reserve provides member banks with lending facilities), or borrowing for speculation or arbitrage, would be considered an inappropriate use of Federal reserve credit.

C. The money market

Q15. Describe the role and assess the significance of accepting houses.

A15. Accepting houses are those merchant banks who are members of the Accepting Houses Committee. They provide acceptance credit by opening accounts for customers, who can then issue bank bills to the value of the credit. The accepting house pays the bills at maturity and debits the customer for the amount, plus commission. Reimbursement credit is acceptance credit opened by a foreign bank with a British bank on behalf of a foreign company. When an accepting house signs its name to a bill, it is, in effect, guaranteeing the amount. This makes the bill more 'acceptable' for discounting into cash and at a lower discount rate. The introduction of the new monetary sector increased the number of banks whose acceptances were eligible for discounting by the Bank of England. First-class bills were no longer issued only by the clearers, accepting houses and major British overseas and Commonwealth banks, but also by a new group of other 'eligible' banks.

The merchant banks have, therefore, developed their other business. They help in the raising of new capital, both domestically and internationally. They organise new issues and mergers; manage unit and investment trusts and deal in certificates of deposit and Eurocurrency transactions. They provide short-term finance, corporate finance and investment advice; they accept deposit/current accounts and are involved in all types of wholesale banking. Those merchant banks who are members of the Accepting Houses Committee help in the flotation of new issues. Some deal in bullion, several deal in commodities and others deal in leasing, export finance and factoring. The latter is a form of debt collecting. The merchant bank buys up a customer's debt for a given sum, or gets paid pro rata on the amount recovered. Because merchant banks have a less rigid structure than the clearing banks and do not have to provide so many retail outlets, their operational costs are generally cheaper and they can often be more flexible in their approach.

Q16. Describe the role and assess the significance of sterling certificates of deposit.

A16. Sterling certificates of deposit are certificates issued by commercial banks for sterling deposits of £5,000 by £1,000 multiples to £500,000 and for specified periods of around 3 months to 5 years. The interest is fixed at the outset, but the certificates can be sold in the parallel money market before the due date, at a price which will fluctuate with the level of interest. They are bearer securities, popular with holders because there is usually an interest rate advantage over ordinary bank deposits, and popular with banks because the money cannot be withdrawn until the end of the term specified, although, as stated above, they can be sold in the parallel market before maturity. The discount houses are mainly the market makers in these securities, although banks are the primary issuers.

Q17. Explain briefly the meaning of 'secured call loans'.

A17. Call loans are loans made by banks to discount houses. They are immediately repayable on call and are secured against assets held by the discount houses, such as Treasury bills, short-term Government stock and certificates of deposit. Since 1981, 'eligible' banks have had to hold at least 4% of their eligible liabilities in secured money with the discount houses each day. This requirement altered in 1983 to 2.5% each day.

Q18. Describe Treasury bills.

A18. Treasury bills first appeared in March 1877 following the passing of the Treasury Bills Act. They are issued as 'tender' or 'tap' bills. Both are bearer securities charged on the Consolidated Fund. 'Tender' bills are issued in the money market with the discount houses being the largest bidders. The Bank of England used to quote prices at which it would buy bills from the discount houses. Since 1980, in pursuance of its aim to influence short-term interest rates, it has discontinued this policy. The discount houses now set the prices they want for their bills. The

Bank then decides which offers to accept. Treasury bills are issued in amounts ranging from £5,000 to £1m with a three-month maturity. The houses do not hold the bills for the whole 90 days but sell them to the banks, usually within one to four weeks after purchase. 'Tap' bills are Treasury bills available for purchase by Government departments or agencies who have a temporary surplus of cash.

Q19. Outline the functions of the London discount market.

A19. Discount houses borrow from the banks at call (call money) and at short notice. They use this borrowed money to provide short-term credit to (a) the public sector by way of Treasury bills and short-term gilts with less than five years to maturity and (b) the private sector by way of commercial bills. As well as providing short-term finance for public and private sectors, the discount market also provides the major secondary market for certificates of deposit. They may even take up some of these certificates when they are first issued by the Bank, and thus become part of the primary market. More often, they deal in them after they have been taken up by other holders. The discount market took on a new importance after the 1981 monetary control measures. The Bank of England wished to use short-term interest rates as a leverage on money supply control. Therefore, there had to be an adequate supply of bills and enough funds for the discount houses to buy them. Their bill-broking activities were assured by the increase in the number of banks whose bills became eligible for re-discount at the Bank of England, and by the requirement that eligible banks had to keep 4% to 6% of their eligible liabilities on an average daily basis in secured money with the discount houses, and/or secured call money with money brokers and gilt-edged jobbers.

Q20. What, briefly, is the sterling inter-bank market?

A20. The sterling inter-bank market is one of the parallel or secondary money markets in London. It is a market through which banks borrow or lend in sterling to each other at rates which vary with conditions in the market. The lending is un-secured; mainly short-term and arranged through brokers, unlike normal overdraft lending, which is the result of direct agreement between the banks concerned. For longer-term trans-actions, sterling certificates of deposit may be used.

Q21. Describe the local authority market in London.

A21. Local authorities were allowed to borrow only from the Public Works Board from 1945 until 1954. They were then encouraged to borrow elsewhere, and so one of the parallel markets in London was born: that of the local authority market, which began in 1955. The biggest authorities with a rate call of £5m can issue bonds in their own name under the Local Government Act 1972, and the Stocks and Bonds Regulations 1974. But borrowing by the local authorities is also short-term. The five main sources of funds are from the Public Works Loan Board acting as lender of last resort; direct from the public usually through advertising; from the money market with the help of brokers; through the stock market with variable and fixed-rate bonds and from overseas.

Local authorities rarely borrow to finance revenue expenditure. They pay these costs (salaries; running expenses; debt servicing) by payments from the Government (including grants), receipts from rents and trading activities and by property taxes (rates). Of capital expenditure, about $7/8$ is financed by borrowing, with the balance coming from revenue, capital receipts and other sources. Temporary or short-term borrowing is raised for less than one year; long-term for more than one year. There are controls on the proportion of short-term to total borrowing and upon the maturity structure both of short-term and fresh longer-term borrowing. By 31 March 1980, local authority external temporary debt amounted to £5,466m, divided among Central Government and public corporations (£682m), banks (£1,070m), other financial institutions (£2,298m) and industrial and commercial companies, personal sector, etc., (£1,416m). None of this sum is marketable and none of the paper issued in receipt changes hands. Local authority longer-term debt amounted to £28,008m.

Topic 9

The Balance of Payments

The structure of the balance of payments and that of the United Kingdom in particular, including an appreciation of recent influences. Causes of changes in the balance; methods of adjusting the balance.

The balance of payments

This is a summarised statement of all the transactions between the United Kingdom and overseas residents which involve a flow of resources such as goods, services, property income, a change in the United Kingdom's foreign assets/liabilities and transfer payments, such as overseas aid, pensions, gifts and subscriptions. In the United Kingdom the statement is divided into four main sections: (1) A trading account which is called the *current account*. (2) A capital account which is called *investment and other capital flows*. (3) A balancing or compensating account which is called the *balancing item*. These three totals are added to give the total flow of currency, known as the *balance for official financing*. In some years, there may be extras to add to or subtract from the currency flow, such as subs. to or SDR's from the International Monetary Fund. (4) The fourth section of the balance of payments is called *official financing*.

The current account

This consists of two parts. The first part is called the *trade* or *visible balance*: the export and import of goods and the export and import of services. It is the balance – credit or debit – achieved after taking into account all the goods exported and imported over the year. The second part of the current account is called the *balance of invisibles*. This is the balance – credit or debit – achieved after taking into account money received or paid for, invisible imports and exports. 'Invisibles' are mainly services. They comprise Government transactions, banking, insurance, tourism and transport by road, sea and air. Fees, royalties and commissions for the use of patents and supplies of films and technical services are also included, as well as profits and dividends. Payments without a quid pro quo, such as money sent to the 'home' country by immigrants, are classed as an invisible export, and some countries rely heavily on such gifts of money from their workers in other countries. Other invisible exports might be pensions and subscriptions to international agencies, such as the IMF and the Common Market. When the earnings from invisible exports exceed the cost of invisible imports, there is a surplus on the invisible balance. This surplus or deficit is added to the net balance of visibles (goods), and the result is the figure for the trade balance.

Investment and other capital flows

This is added to the current account and involves the flow of capital by means of loans, investment and bank deposits. Such capital can be lent or borrowed by Governments or individuals. Direct investment occurs when a United Kingdom company purchases shares in a foreign company and exercises control over that company. Indirect investment is the purchase of shares in a company without exercising control over that company.

The balancing item

Sometimes the figures do not exactly match because of time lags. Thus, people leaving the United Kingdom in December of one year and spending their money overseas will probably not have this outflow of capital recorded in the balance of payments until the following year. A balancing item is therefore entered in the balance of payments statement. Entries in the balancing item represent the cumulative totals of items that have gone unrecorded up to that point. The balancing item, the current account and the capital account are added together. The total, credit or debit, is the balance for official financing and is accommodated by the official financing section.

The official financing section

If current and capital accounts show a total credit, e.g., of £1,000m, the official financing section will show a debit of £1,000m. This means that the credit has been used for repayment of debt incurred in earlier years, or that the amount has been added to the foreign currency reserves. If the current and capital accounts show a debit balance, e.g., of £1,000m, this means that the United Kingdom has paid £1,000m more out to non-residents than it has had in from them. The official financing section will thus show a £1,000m credit item: money taken from the reserves to finance the debt, or borrowed from international monetary organisations.

Changes in the balance of payments

Changes occur in the balance of payments because of changes in the demand for capital and goods of different countries at different times. A debit balance can be corrected by greater earnings of foreign currency, financed by borrowing from the reserves or overseas. This is not easy. A depreciation of the home currency makes imports dearer and exports cheaper. In theory this should lead to higher net earnings, but much depends on the relative elasticities of demand for exports and imports. A higher price for goods and services with an inelastic demand usually means a higher total revenue for those goods and services; a higher price with an elastic demand means less of the product will be bought, and, in general, total revenue from its sale will fall. Methods for remedying a current account deficit other than a depreciation of the currency could include implicit restrictions on imports (e.g., by making the rules and regulations for importers very rigorous or difficult) or explicit restrictions by quotas and similar embargoes. Exports could be stimulated by sales drives. In extreme cases, rationing of certain goods for home consumption might be imposed in order to increase exports.

A deficit is financed, but not cured, by borrowing from the reserves or from overseas monetary institutions, such as the International Monetary Fund, or else by gifts. Such a policy cannot continue indefinitely. If the deficit is not remedied, the currency will have to be devalued if it is on a fixed exchange rate, or it will fall to a very low level if it is on a floating rate. The fall will have the effect of lowering the purchasing power of the country's currency and make imports so costly to buy that their volume, and the deficit balance, will be reduced.

Countries often try to correct a deficit in their current balance of payments by allowing the value of their currency to depreciate on the foreign exchange market. The terms of trade are the ratio of export to import prices. The ratio is calculated by using the following formula:

$$\frac{\text{index of export prices} \times 100}{\text{index of import prices}}$$

A base year is used from which to make the calculation. If in year one the terms are, for example, 100 and in year two they are 125, a favourable balance of trade is said to exist: the prices of exports are high relative to the prices of imports. If in year two the terms of trade are 90, they are 'unfavourable'.

Depreciation of a currency means allowing its exchange rate to fall against another. If £1 = $2 and then depreciates to $1.50, the £ can buy fewer United States goods and the $ can buy more British goods. Imports fall, exports rise; more dollars come in, fewer pounds flow out – but this scenario depends entirely on the elasticity of demand for both exports and imports. After depreciation to $1.50, the sale of 100 British goods, which formerly brought in $200, will now bring in only $150. Unless at least another 34 goods can be sold, there will be a fall in revenue. There must also be spare capacity to produce the goods. Demand for imports must similarly be elastic, so that the higher prices deter buyers. If not, other measures may have to be taken to offset the effect of rising import prices. These could include wage or price controls, rationing and/or fiscal monetary measures. Without the right export/import elasticity and the capacity to produce more goods, depreciation will not improve the balance of payments. Its first effect will in any event usually be adverse, because more has to be paid immediately for imports and less is received for exports (the J curve).

Questions on the balance of payments

(Note to student: some sections of the syllabus need memorising. Some topics such as the balance of payments and exchange rates need rather an understanding of the principles involved, although an ability to recall export and import figures or to know current exchange rates for the major currencies is never a disadvantage.)

Q1. In what sense do a country's balance of payments' accounts always balance? How will the operation of a freely floating exchange rate regime affect the balance for official financing?

A1. The balance of payments is an account in financial terms of one country's trading with another over a period of time. It consists of three main items and a balancing item, which reflects omissions and errors of previous years. The current balance is made up of the balance of visibles (payments for goods) and the balance of invisibles (payments for services). The capital account shows the movement of capital. A balancing item makes adjustments for items that come in late. When the total of investment and other capital flows is added to the current account balance it gives the balance for official financing. The balance of payments always 'balances', because official financing (the same total) makes up any deficit or uses up any credit.

A credit balance for official financing shows a surplus on the balance of payments. This is used to pay debts, and is paid into the official reserves or to international monetary institutions. The balance for official financing will appear as a negative figure in the column known as official financing. When the sum of the current and capital accounts, adjusted by the balancing item, is negative, this means that there is an overall deficit on the balance of payments, which will have to be financed. A credit item of the same amount will go in the official financing column. It shows from what institution(s) money has been borrowed to cover the deficit. In this way, the balance of payments always balances: the official financing column always transfers a surplus to official reserves or similar accounts, or else shows from what source a deficit has been financed.

When a freely floating exchange rate operates, there is no need to keep large reserves. The exchange rate does not need support. In theory, a balance for official financing is unnecessary. When more payments flow out than flow into a country, the supply of its currency increases and its exchange rate will depreciate. The exchange rate will adjust the current account balance with that of the capital account. Any balance for official financing will tend to be small, and due mainly to sudden changes in the exchange rate. With freely floating exchange rates, public and private sector operators are likely to deal in the forward market to offset the uncertainties of international trade. Such dealings will create surpluses or deficits in both capital and current accounts, and some measure of official financing may take place. In practice, few countries leave exchange rate fluctuations completely at the mercy of market forces. They will intervene if the rate is moving too high or too low.

Q2. Analyse the changes that have taken place in the balance of payments on current account of a developing country with which you are acquainted.
(Note to student: questions on changing trends in the balance of payments usually refer to a given time period. The student is expected to know the trends and their effect on the balance of payments of the particular country.)

A2. Developing countries usually have poor resources in relation to the number of people. The per capita income is very low, with agriculture as the main source of livelihood and little or no industry. Machines, tools and similar capital goods will all have to be imported. The current account is usually in deficit, with constant borrowing to keep the economy 'going'. Little help comes from the richer nations, as the Brandt Report emphasised. The discovery of a new resource fundamentally changes the balance of payments of a developing country. Not only do exports increase; so do imports. Consumption increases and capital goods are wanted in large quantities. The current account figures will reflect this increase. The balance may still be in deficit because the desire for goods may precede the development of the new resource. But foreign currency coming into the country for investment (when allowed) will boost the capital account.

Q3. What do you understand by the 'invisibles' section of a country's balance of payments accounts? Assess the importance of any recent influences on the invisibles account of the United Kingdom or any other country with which you are familiar.

A3. The invisibles section of a country's balance of payments is detailed in the introduction to this topic. Note that dividends and interest go into the invisibles account; the capital flows that generate them go into the capital (investment and other capital flows) account. Note also that the invisibles account includes transfers of funds by Government as well as individuals, so that payments by the United Kingdom to the EEC are included in this section, but grants from the EEC will go into the capital account. The United Kingdom has traditionally had a balance of invisibles surplus, which has often made up for the deficit on the trade balance.

Influences on the United Kingdom invisibles account include the following factors, but specific results depend on the period in question: (a) the exchange rate and its effect on tourism, etc.; (b) investments by overseas companies in North Sea oil production or other United Kingdom resources, and resulting payment of dividends and profits overseas; (c) any restrictions on the movement of currency such as exchange control, which limits the movement of funds, and the associated movement (creation) of dividends, interest and profit; and (d) any treaties, Government agreements, etc., which involve transfer payments such as those paid to the EEC. (Note the difference between transfers and flows: the former is like a gift – there is no quid pro quo. A flow of capital creates a payment and goes into the investment account.)

Q4. 'The external receipts and payments of a country, in total, must balance.' Explain this statement, illustrating your answer with reference to the United Kingdom.

A4. The external receipts and payments in the United Kingdom always balance, in the same way that any bookkeeping transaction must always balance. When goods or services are sold they are paid for or credit is given. In the latter case, the flow of capital to cover the credit will be shown in the capital account. This account adds up all the flows of capital coming in and out of the country for investment or for borrowing by Governments and individuals. Official financing covers any deficit on the totals of trading and capital accounts by borrowing the requisite sum and transfering any surplus to the reserves. The balancing item shown in the accounts adjusts the discrepancies due to time lags or difficulties in identifying particular items. The balance of payments always balances because any deficit is 'paid' by borrowing. Any credit or deficit on the balance of payments will be offset by a balancing amount in the official financing column.

Q5. Distinguish between (a) terms of trade and (b) balance of trade. How is a country's balance of trade affected by changes in its terms of trade?

A5. The terms of trade are the ratio of export to import prices (see above). The balance of trade is the total of export earnings for 'visibles' (goods) minus the total of import payments for such items, over a period of time. Both are measured as free on board (fob), which means their value on shipment including any expenses to that point. A country's balance of trade is affected by changes in its terms of trade because the latter reflect price changes in imports and exports. If export prices fall, more will have to be sold to compensate for the lower margin on each, unless import demand falls correspondingly. This will not happen if import demand is inelastic.

If the volume of imports and exports remains unchanged, then unfavourable terms of trade will lead to a deterioration in the balance of trade. Favourable terms, with volumes similarly unchanged, will mean a credit balance. In the long run the balance of trade will depend on the elasticities of supply and demand. (*See also* answer 4 above.) Exports and imports must have an elastic demand, and supply must be able to expand to meet any increased export demand.

Q6. In what circumstances may an improvement in a country's terms of trade not be advantageous?

A6. The terms of trade compare changes in the prices of a country's imports and exports over a period of time. There are several ways of measuring these changes. The simplest is to take the export index of a year and divide it by the import index. If both indices are at 100 the formula will look like this:

$$\frac{\text{export price index}}{\text{import price index}} \times 100 = 100$$

If import prices fall by 10% but export prices remain unchanged, the formula would look like this:

$$\frac{100}{90} \times 100 = 111$$

The higher figures show that terms have moved favourably: more imports can be exchanged for the same amount of exports. Such an 'improvement' may not always be advantageous, however. Total revenue must improve, and this depends on the elasticities of demand for imports and exports. If prices of exports rise relative to imports (improvement in the terms of trade), but less exports are bought (elastic demand) and a compensating fall in imports does not take place, then the country's total revenue will also fall. Therefore, an improvement in the terms of trade will not be advantageous when there is an elastic demand for exports and imports. The demand for primary products is often inelastic, whereas demand for manufactured goods is more often elastic. The revenue of a developing nation is, therefore, particularly affected by the price structure of the goods it buys and sells.

Q7. The figures below in Table 6.1 are taken from the annual balance of payments of Ruritania. Prepare (a) Ruritania's balance of visible trade and (b) Ruritania's balance of payments on current account. Do these figures support the contention that Ruritania is a developing country and not highly industrialised? Give reasons for your answer.

Table 6.1

	Million rurits
Banking earnings (net)	−30
Capital movements (net inflow)	+1280
Insurance earnings (net)	−20
Interest paid abroad	−1400
Interest received from abroad	+30
Manufactured goods	
exports (fob)	+120
imports (fob)	−2000
Raw materials and fuel	
exports (fob)	+3000
imports (fob)	−1000
Shipping earnings (net)	−80
Tourist earnings (net)	+100

There were no changes in Ruritania's official reserves during the year.

(Note to student: although this question was set some time ago, it is a good one for revision as it tests understanding of the principles involved.)

A7. (a) Table 6.2

Ruritania's balance of visible trade

	Dr	Cr
Manufactured goods: exports		120
imports	2000	
Raw materials and fuel: exports		3000
imports	1000	
	3000	3120

Surplus of 120 rurits (m) on the balance of trade

(b)
Table 6.3

Balance of invisibles		
	Dr (m)	Cr (m)
Banking earnings (net)	30	
Insurance earnings (net)	20	
Interest paid	1400	
Interest received		30
Shipping earnings (net)	80	
Tourist earnings		100
	1530	130

Deficit of 1400 rurits (m)
Current account balance = surplus on trade of   120 m rurits
Current account balance = deficit on invisibles of 1400 m rurits
Current account balance = overall deficit of   1280 m rurits

The figures support the view that Ruritania is a developing country. Manufactured exports are very low; imports are high. There is a large reliance on the export of primary products, which is typical of many developing countries. So, too, is the small volume of invisible exports, e.g., banking and insurance. Tourism is small, but the largest 'invisible' earner, and this is again fairly typical of developing countries (except for the poorest). Borrowing is not confined to developing countries but the balance of payments here shows very large interest payments, with very little incoming flow from this source; whereas developed countries, though often large borrowers, show high interest payments coming in too.

Topic 10

Exchange Rates

Fixed and floating exchange rates. The European Monetary System, intervention points and support arrangements. The exchange equalisation account and leads and lags. A comparison of the differing types of exchange rate.

What is an exchange rate?

An exchange rate is a price paid in one currency for another. If £1 buys $2, the exchange rate for $1 is 50p (£1/2). The two main types of exchange rate are fixed and floating. When a fixed rate is in operation, the country has a rate fixed to a certain unchanging value point: a par value, such as existed when the value for an ounce of gold varied only by the change in the cost of transporting the gold from one country to another. All the countries which entered the Bretton Woods Agreement of 1944 had fixed rates with a 1% band above and below a fixed dollar parity. The dollar itself was fixed in value to an ounce of gold, so that all the countries in the system were related both to the dollar and to gold. This changed in 1971–2 when floating rates were adopted. The Common Market countries formed their own 'snake': a floating rate within a fixed band, from which developed the present European Monetary System.

Floating and fixed rates each have certain advantages and disadvantages. Fixed rates provide certainty in international transactions. Their main disadvantage is that large reserves must be kept to support the rate when there is a drain on the currency.

Furthermore, the need to keep to the fixed rate can conflict with domestic economic policy.

The European Monetary System

(No questions have been set on this topic but since the subject is part of the syllabus dealing with exchange rates the following outline is given.)

The EMS came into force in March 1979. All five members of the existing snake, Belgium, Denmark, Holland, Luxemburg and West Germany, stayed in and were joined by France, Ireland and Italy but not the United Kingdom. The idea of the EMS was to establish a stable monetary zone with greater harmonisation of financial and economic policies. The system is like the snake, in that it has a central rate for each currency. This central rate is set in terms of the European currency unit (ecu) which is based on a basket of members' currencies, weighted according to their economic importance in the EEC. Sterling is included in the basket although the United Kingdom did not join the EMS. The ecu: (a) is the denominator for the exchange rate mechanism, (b) acts as the basis for the divergence indicator, (c) is the denominator for operations in the intervention and credit mechanisms and (d) acts as a means of settlement between the monetary authorities of the EEC.

Intervention points

Each country kept within a margin of 2.25% either side of the central rate, except for Italy, which had a margin of roughly 6% either side of its rate of 466.5 lire, with an upper intervention limit of 495.3 and a lower intervention limit of 430.3. When a country reaches either the top or bottom intervention point, it must intervene to prevent the currency falling below or going above the limits set. There is also a divergence indicator. This gives warning that intervention may be needed in the near future. The EMS is a great improvement on the snake because of: (a) the divergence indicator, (b) the substantial credit-support facilities which are available and (c) the ability to realign a currency when required, e.g., the Deutschmark was revalued in 1979 by 2% against most of the currencies in the EMS and by 5% against the Danish krone.

Support arrangements

These include a very short-term facility which provides almost unlimited support for up to ten weeks with a further automatic three months if needed. The facilities can be extended further by agreement. There is also short-term monetary support of around ecu 14bn for up to nine months. Each member country has a borrowing ceiling and a commitment ceiling, with the latter twice as high as the former. Finally, there is medium-term financial assistance of ecu 11bn available for members in balance of payments difficulties, plus, if required, credits extended for three to five years subject to economic policy decisions imposed by the Council of Ministers. The administration of the support facilities is done through the European Monetary Co-operation Fund. Members deposit 20% of their gold holdings and 20% of their United States dollar holdings against an equivalent issue of ecus, which are then used between members in settlement of debt.

The exchange equalisation account

Set up in 1932 after Britain left the gold standard (1931), the exchange equalisation account was meant to smoothe out short-term fluctuations in the exchange value of sterling. In 1939, the gold and convertible currencies held by the Bank of England were transferred to the account. It is managed by the Bank which buys or sells sterling: to keep sterling within prescribed limits during a fixed exchange rate regime, or to smooth out temporary aberrations in the rate when the currency is floating.

Leads and lags

Leads and lags take place when a country's exchange rate is expected to change. If, for example, sterling is expected to fall, importers will speed up their sales of sterling and their purchases of foreign currencies. They know that the longer they delay, the more likely is the value of sterling to fall. They are the leads: the early buyers or sellers. On the other hand, exporters will find that payments to them lag behind. The longer the lag, the more sterling will be ultimately received for their foreign currency. When a currency is expected to go up, the effects will be the other way. Thus, if sterling is expected to rise, importers will delay in buying foreign currency. They will get more for their pounds later. Exporters will find their customers rushing to pay bills. The longer those customers delay paying, the less sterling they will receive for their foreign currency. Leads and lags can have big effects on exchange rates and reserves, particularly during a regime of fixed exchange rates, or rates operating within a narrow band. In 1976 when sterling was depreciating, leads and lags moved against the United Kingdom. In 1977 when sterling was strong, the position was reversed.

Fixed versus floating exchange rates

The fixed rate system which operated between the major world currencies under the Bretton Woods system had certain inherent disadvantages, but survived for 25 years, up to 1971. The main problems were: (a) the inability of countries to devalue/realign their currencies quickly enough to avoid speculation; (b) reserve currencies, such as sterling, could suffer heavy withdrawals from their reserves due to events in countries that kept their balances in the United Kingdom; (c) insufficient liquidity for world trade, or so it was thought, although the problem was more one of the quality of liquidity than its adequacy; (d) there was no (and perhaps could not be any) penalty for countries with a continual surplus on their balance of payments; (e) speculation, which constantly took place when countries were seen to be about to revalue or devalue their currencies. Finally, (f) a return to a fixed rate system needed a large majority of the IMF members in favour, which was not the case.

The arguments for the return to a system of floating rates can be summed up as follows: (a) more attention can be given to domestic issues without the constraint of a fixed exchange rate and (b) there is no need for excessive reserves. The arguments against are: (a) instability; (b) hindrance to trade and (c) domestic policies, which may have to be framed to take account of the balance of payments.

In practical rather than theoretical terms, there were strong forces working against the return of fixed rates. Countries have different inflation rates leading to large flows of capital across national borders, and it is not easy to harmonise domestic and external policies when the exchange rate is fixed and needs large reserves for support. The fixed rate system provides certainty in international trade, but reserves must be kept and domestic policies pursued (sometimes unwisely) to support the rate. Floating rates give more flexibility but less discipline. The factors which led to the breakdown of the fixed rate system, namely differences in inflation rates and balances of payments in different countries, still exist. However, the European Monetary System has kept going. The upper and lower limits for intervention are wide enough, particularly in the case of Italy, to allow for some degree of flexibility between the points. The obligation to intervene by 'strong' as well as 'weak' currency countries has given the system a stability that has surprised many of its earlier critics.

Table 7: Summary of the advantages and disadvantages of different types of exchange rate

Advantages	Disadvantages
(A) Floating rates	
1. Market mechanism adjusts currency price and establishes payments equilibrium	Future price uncertainty may cause traders to: (a) lessen their international trade (b) buy forward cover (c) speculate
2. World trade encouraged by the freedom from control	Expensive forward cover inhibits international trade
3. Freedom for domestic policies	Irresponsible domestic policies can be pursued without regard to future prospects or falls in the exchange rate
4. Lessens the need for a large volume of international liquidity	Intervention still needed to smoothe out excessive short-term changes in the exchange rate
5. No need for large reserves	Controls on capital movements are still enforced under a floating rate system
(B) Fixed rates (gold standard)	
1. Stability in international trade, investment and domestic policies	Restricts freedom on domestic policies
2. Encourages international economic integration	Gold supply is too limited for international trade, or it may be restricted for political reasons
3. Any loss of reserves causes corrective action and prevents inflation. Further, a gold monetary base is not as easily expanded as is a paper or bookkeeping one	Gold acts as a reserve currency

Fixed rates (Bretton Woods)

1. Easy to understand	Causes delays in exchange rate adjustments
2. Provides discipline	Speculation encouraged by chance of devaluation
3. Price certainty in international trade	Large reserves needed, or ability to borrow
4. Encourages international economic integration	Domestic policies impeded by need to watch reserves
	Inflation (over consumption) encouraged when deficits financed by borrowing
	Deficit countries must devalue; surplus countries (often) do not revalue

(C) Flexible rates (crawling peg)

1. Allows for adjustment but gives certainty: high interest rates for depreciating currencies; low for appreciating ones	Control of interest rates can deter long-term investment
2. Restricts speculation	

Questions on exchange rates

Q1. Explain briefly the possible effect on the supply of day to day credit when large purchases of sterling are made by the authorities to support the rate for sterling in the foreign exchange market.

(Note to student: although this question applies to a system of fixed rates, there are occasions with a floating exchange rate when the authorities intervene in the market to keep their exchange rate to what is thought to be the desired level. The answer below gives the mechanics of this intervention.)

A1. When the authorities purchase (support) sterling they sell foreign currencies from the reserves. The sterling is supplied by the foreign exchange market through the dealing banks. The banks are also the main suppliers of funds to the money (discount) market. Having supplied sterling to the Bank, they have less call money for the discount houses. The Bank of England can supply the houses with funds at a penal rate if it wishes credit to remain tight, or else at any other rate it chooses. A further squeeze on day to day credit is a result of fewer Treasury bills on the market. This is because a purchase of sterling by the authorities results in a transfer of assets from the exchange equalisation account to the National Loans Fund for tap bills. The NLF has, therefore, less need to raise money through the sale of Treasury bills to the market. Day to day credit will correspondingly come under pressure.

Q2. Why has the international system of fixed exchange rates which has operated since the Second World War been widely replaced by floating rates?

A2. The fixed rate system of exchange rates which had been in operation since 1946 broke down in 1971. Most rates were fixed in terms of the dollar, which itself had a par value of $35 an ounce of gold. Persistent United States payments deficits meant that dollar holders were anxious to change their dollars into other currencies. This flight from the dollar undermined the fixed rate system. In August 1971, the United States suspended the convertibility of the dollar into gold at the fixed rate of $35 an ounce. In December 1971, at the Smithsonian meeting in Washington, the ten countries participating in the general arrangements to borrow (the 'Group of Ten') agreed to a realignment of currencies with new 'central rates' to the United States dollar.

Shortly afterwards, the United States dollar was devalued in terms of gold to $35 an ounce: an increase in the gold price of 8.57%. Sterling could not uphold the unrealistic new 'central rate' of £ = $2.6057 and floated in June 1972. Other currencies followed suit. The large increases in oil prices, which came a few years later with the attendant problem of recycling money flows, prevented any return to a fixed rate system of exchange rates. The EEC made an attempt at a fixed rate system with a margin of fluctuation (the 'snake'), and later adopted the European Monetary System. This has the elements of a fixed exchange rate, but with intervention points where the countries belonging to the system have to take action to support or depress a currency that is temporarily out of alignment.

Q3. Outline the principles on which a central bank operates in the foreign exchange market when (a) it is formally committed to maintaining the exchange rate of its currency within narrow limits and (b) when it is not.

A3. (a) The principles on which a central bank operates in the foreign exchange market, when it is formally committed to maintaining the exchange rate of its currency, are that it must buy its own currency when the exchange rate reaches the lowest limit and sell when it reaches the highest. It can only buy its own currency if it has other currencies available or can borrow them. When the exchange rate is between the upper and lower limits, the central bank may intervene or not as it thinks fit. If it intervenes, the reason may be to acquire a large surplus of foreign currency for later support use.

(b) The principles on which a central bank operates on the foreign exchange, when it is not formally committed to maintaining the exchange rate, are to ensure a reasonable equilibrium, buying its own currency when its exchange rate is low and selling when it is high. Such intervention is known as a 'dirty float'.

Q4. How and why do central banks intervene in the foreign exchange markets?

A4. A central bank usually holds its country's reserves of foreign currencies in a special account, such as the United Kingdom's exchange equilisation account managed by the Bank of England. The central bank can buy or sell its own currency to or from other countries' central banks. It also supplies, at a price, foreign currency to its domestic banks. Buying its own currency will strengthen a country's exchange rate; selling will depreciate it.

The purpose of such intervention is to alter the exchange rate or the level and type of exchange reserves. The rate may have been agreed by international arrangement, such as Bretton Woods, or the European Monetary System. Intervention is meant to adjust the current rate to reflect more accurately the changed real value of the currency. Intervention is also used to affect export/import ratios, encouraging the former; deterring the latter. However, such adjustments are not likely to be effective against market forces created by a floating exchange rate. These forces indicate the demand/supply relationship of various currencies. Any fixed rate that does not reflect these forces cannot survive in the long run, and (other than exchange control) stronger measures such as revaluation or devaluation will be needed to restore the exchange rate to its true parity.

Q5. In the absence of official intervention in the foreign exchange market, what factors are likely to influence changes in a country's exchange rate?

A5. When there is no official intervention in the foreign exchange market, market forces will determine a country's exchange rate. Demand for a country's currency depends on the demand for that country's goods, services and capital. Demand for the goods depends in turn mainly on the quality and price. (Other factors such as reliability of delivery dates can be ignored here.) If the country has high inflation, the price is likely to restrict exports unless the demand for them is relatively inelastic. High interest rates encourage capital to flow into a country. This strengthens its exchange rate, unless the high interest rates indicate pessimistic expectations about future levels of inflation or production.

To summarise, the factors that influence changes in a country's exchange rate (i.e., the supply of and demand for its currency) will be influenced by the following factors: (a) comparative inflation and interest rates, (b) the balance of payments position, (c) expectations of future trends, (d) the monetary and fiscal policy being pursued in a country at any given time and (d) political stability or lack of it; change, or impending change of Government.

Q6. Describe the role and assess the significance of the European Investment Bank.

A6. The European Investment Bank is a non-profit-making public institution set up under the Treaty of Rome 1958, to help the 'balanced development' of the Common Market. It makes loans or guarantees finance for projects which help create jobs in the less developed regions of Europe. Member states provide the funds by subscription. Capital is also raised on the world's capital markets by the sale of bonds. As well as aiding regional development, Article 130 of the Treaty of Rome spelled out two other policy objectives: modernisation and new technology, and projects of common interest to member countries. An example of the former was a new bottling plant set up in the north of England; an example of the latter was the Eurobus project.

The role of the EIB can be summed up as one that contributes to the balanced development of the Common Market. The Bank's loans range between 2 and 10m units of account and for periods of 7–12 years, sometimes even for 20 years. Interest rates are those which prevail in the market where the Bank borrows, and 40% of the cost of the project is usually covered. The significance of the EIB is in its unifying effect on the Common Market, its use of the European unit of account for its calculations and its possible future strength with the development of the European Monetary System.

Topic 11

Eurocurrency Markets

Definition of a Eurocurrency and the Eurocurrency market. The Eurobond market and its financial centres in the world.

A Eurocurrency

A Eurocurrency is any currency operating for loan and repayment outside the country of origin. Eurosterling is bought and sold outside Britain; Eurodollars outside the United States. The latter are dollar deposits in non-American banks and the largest trading currency in the market, which developed in the late 1950s. American banks were then limited in the amount of interest they could pay their depositors and the United States balance of payments deficits meant that large amounts of dollars were held by overseas holders. These holdings were lent and re-lent at higher rates of interest than could be obtained in the United States. Thus the Eurodollar market began.

The Eurodollar market

Today this is very large and is used by Governments, international monetary agencies, public and private corporations and rich individuals. There is no system of international surveillance over the amount of Eurocurrency transactions; nor is there any central bank to which the market can have recourse. The market is a short-term one with deposits lent through a system of bank credits. There is complete freedom from control by the central banks of origin, which gives the market its competitive edge but also the risk inherent in any financial institution that has no lender of last resort.

The origin of the market was due to three factors: (a) Regulation Q prevented United States banks from bidding up interest rates, so that dollars went abroad for higher returns; (b) United Kingdom exchange control 1947–79 prevented the financing of foreign trade in sterling. Treasury restrictions on sterling loans caused banks to borrow in dollars; and (c) the United States balance of payments deficits caused a flow of dollars into banks abroad and so into non-resident hands. Professor Sayers in his book *Money*, gives a further reason: Russian agencies who acquired dollars after the Second World War lent them short-term to West European banks, who further lent them, and so on.

The main operators in the market are multinational corporations, overseas-based companies, commercial banks who exchange local currencies into dollars and similar institutions who have or need different currencies. *The Eurobond market* deals in the long end of the market.

The Eurobond

A Eurobond is a bearer security denominated in any Euro-currency required, which need not be that of the lender or borrower. It is underwritten and distributed by an international syndicate of banks and investment institutions. Most of these belong to the Association of International Bond Dealers, a voluntary association of market participants set up as a self-regulatory agency in 1969.

The Eurobonds may be of different types: fixed, floating or convertible. On fixed-rate bonds the interest is fixed at the time of issue. It is paid annually, and dealt in on a plus or minus accrued interest based on a 360-day year and a 30-day month. Floating rate bonds have interest based on calendar months.

Financial centres

London is the largest centre for the Eurobond market with 34%, but Paris remains the main centre for Eurosterling. Other Euro-currency markets are in Amsterdam, Frankfurt and Zurich. Singapore is the main centre in the East. There are also financial centres in Bahrain, Hong Kong, Panama, the Bahamas and the Cayman Islands.

Questions on Eurocurrency markets

Q1. Account for the growth of the Eurocurrency markets. Is there a case for international control of these markets?

A1. The reasons for the growth of the Eurocurrency markets can be summed up as follows: restrictions by monetary authorities on domestic market rates to achieve various policy objectives, higher interest rates generally prevailing in Euromarkets on deposits and lower interest rates generally available on loans. Payment of interest on Eurodeposits is made gross without deduction of tax, is payable to bearer and can be made in a choice of currencies. The case for international control is strong, and monitoring and surveillance by the World Bank and the BIS is not enough to prevent some banks from getting into difficulties. However, efforts at prudential regulation on a world basis are unlikely to bear much fruit.

Q2. To what extent have the Eurocurrency markets helped in overcoming the problems posed for international liquidity requirements by the large balance of payments surpluses of the oil-producing countries in recent years?

A2. Large surpluses mean that some countries have large deficits. Surpluses deposited in the Eurocurrency markets were recycled to countries in deficit. International liquidity problems were thereby overcome in the short term, although the longer-term problem of international debt was left unsolved.

Q3. Why are rates of interest paid on deposits in the Euromarkets usually higher than comparable rates paid on domestic deposits? How far does this factor explain the rapid growth in the Euromarkets?

(Note to student: you are being asked to decide if higher interest rates on deposits explains the growth of the Euromarkets. Efforts at, or reasons for, control of the market are not being asked for. They are included in this answer for information only.)

A3. Euromarkets are markets for bank loans and deposits denominated in a currency outside the country of origin. The Euro prefix derives from the fact that the main markets for such currency originated in Europe. Higher rates of interest can be paid on deposits in Euromarkets, with loans costing less because Euromarkets lack the control and restrictions operating in the various domestic markets. There are no reserve requirements, and no lender of last resort facilities. The World Bank monitors the borrowing of developing countries but not Soviet bloc nations. The Bank for International Settlements records the overseas liabilities and assets of the banks of developed nations and provides the secretariat for a committee of central bank supervisors. However, these arrangements have not prevented overborrowing, e.g., by Poland, Mexico and Zaire; or quite large banks getting into difficulties, e.g., Herstatt in Germany.

The rapid growth of the Euromarkets has been due to several factors. Large depositors (central banks holding reserves of foreign currencies, multinational companies, investment institutions, rich individuals and oil-exporting countries) wanted to earn more on their lending than was possible at home. Their demand for a more sophisticated international capital market coincided with the emergence of a new source of funds. Supply and demand grew up together. No one cause was responsible. Thus, the growth of the Eurosterling market was partly a result of the 'corset' on United Kingdom resident banks. The United Kingdom banks had an incentive to minimise their interest-bearing eligible liabilities. Credit demands were channelled to overseas subsidiaries operating outside the special supplementary deposit ('corset') controls. These overseas subsidiaries could offer higher interest rates for deposits, because they had no need for the reserve assets which were then part of the United Kingdom monetary control provisions. United States depositors also went outside for higher interest rates, because of the interest rate ceilings levied by Regulation Q on deposits at home. Euromarket deposits lacked the restrictions and controls of domestic banks, so their interest rates were higher than those of other deposit takers. An added attractive factor for overseas portfolio managers was that interest is paid gross on Eurobonds, in bearer form, and in a variety of credits. Higher interest does not alone account for the growth of the Euromarket, but it is a significant factor today.

Q4. What are 'offshore banking centres'?
A4. Offshore banking centres are banking centres which have grown in areas outside the traditional ones for financial institutions. The impetus to their growth has usually arisen from three causes: (a) the desire to obtain some tax advantage not available in the 'home' country; (b) some financial gain such as higher interest rates on deposits or lower interest rates on loans

not available in the 'home' country; and (c) the growth of the Eurocurrency market. As it is impossible to have, for example, a Eurosterling market in London, Eurocurrency centres have grown up abroad and offshore banking centres have captured a part of that market. The leading centres are in the Bahamas and the Cayman Isles, Singapore, Hong Kong, Bahrain and Dubai. Financial institutions developed a large number of offshore funds to 'roll up' the yearly income and enable depositors to take their profits in less onerous (tax-wise) capital gains. The Inland Revenue discounted this 'concession' in 1984, so that depositors in offshore funds could no longer 'roll up' dividends for capital growth, but had to accept that dividends, whether taken or not, were income to be taxed as such. The significance of the offshore banking centres is that they provide a very competitive and sophisticated market for (mainly) short-term funds.

Topic 12

International Liquidity

Definition of liquidity and the gold standard. The International Monetary Fund, including quotas and special drawing rights.

International liquidity

Liquidity gives its owner immediate purchasing power. International liquidity does the same on an international scale. It is defined by the International Monetary Fund as the total means of payments acceptable for international settlements over which the monetary authorities have immediate and unconditional command.

The components of international liquidity

The components of international liquidity are gold and convertible foreign currencies, special drawing rights and official borrowing facilities held with the IMF. These amounts are quantifiable, and exclude borrowing arrangements between individual countries that, for all sorts of reasons, may not be taken up.

Gold, once very important as an international reserve, declined in importance during the 1950s and 1960s, a reflection of its fixed official price and limited supply. In 1975 IMF members no longer had to pay 25% of their quotas in gold, and the IMF began selling off its holdings of gold at market-related prices. By the 1980s, because of its market-related price, gold comprised some 50% of international reserves, compared with only 9.6%

valued at the fixed official price. Some further importance was given to gold as a reserve asset by EEC members having to pay a proportion of gold and reserve currencies into the European Monetary Co-operation Fund and receiving European currency units (ecus) in return.

The gold standard

The gold standard was a fixed exchange rate system, which continued from the early 19th century in the United Kingdom to 1914, and thereafter in a somewhat different form, until 1931 when the United Kingdom's gold was transferred to the Exchange Equalisation Fund, later named the Exchange Equalisation Account. Three conditions were needed for a full gold standard: (a) the unit of account had to be a fixed weight of gold. The £ equalled 0.257 standard ounces of gold; (b) paper money had to be freely convertible into gold, but there was no need for gold coins to circulate; (c) no import or export restrictions could be placed on gold.

The United Kingdom came off this full gold standard at the outbreak of World War One. In 1925 it returned to a 'gold bullion' standard. Gold was obtainable from the Bank of England only in bars of 400 ounces at a price of around £1,600. This system was given up in 1931 and the gold was transferred to the EEA. In 1944 at Bretton Woods, a gold exchange standard was fixed for all the members of the IMF. The countries had an exchange rate fixed to the United States dollar, which was itself convertible into gold at the price of $35 per ounce. In 1964, the Ossola Report recommended the use of SDRs ('paper gold'). In 1968 a two-tier system for gold was introduced: a free market price and an official price. In 1968 SDRs were approved, and distributed over the period 1970–81. The United States had meanwhile introduced non-convertibility of the dollar in August 1971, and in 1972 raised the official price of gold against the dollar from $35 an ounce to $38 an ounce. In 1973, new crises caused a run on the dollar and the official price of gold for transactions between monetary authorities was raised to $44.22 an ounce.

The market price continued to rise and in order to offset this, the IMF embarked on a series of auctions of its gold. One sixth of the proceeds went to help developing countries and one sixth was returned to members. The gold sales had little effect on the market price of gold. It continued to rise as oil-producing countries, considering gold a better store of value than depreciating currencies, bought more of the yellow metal. The gold price touched £800 an ounce in 1979, fell in 1980 when sterling became a stronger currency, and by 1983 was below $400. Efforts to demonetise gold had a slight set-back with the creation of the European currency unit in 1979. Members of the EEC had to pay a proportion of gold (valued at a market-related price) and reserve holdings into the European Monetary Co-operation Fund in return for ecus. Gold continues to attract holders because it can be used as a medium of exchange, but unlike other media it also serves, in times of inflation, as a good store of value.

Institutions providing international liquidity

The institutions which help to provide international liquidity on a global scale are the International Monetary Fund, its affiliate institutions and, by the recycling of funds, the Eurocurrency markets. The European Monetary System has also added to world liquidity by its very limited re-monetisation of gold.

The International Monetary Fund

This was established at a meeting in Bretton Woods, the United States of America, in 1944, to promote international monetary co-operation. The Fund's Articles of Agreement, which constitute an international treaty, set out the purposes of the Fund, which are: (1) to promote international monetary co-operation through a permanent institution. (2) To facilitate the expansion and balanced growth of world trade and thereby to promote and maintain high levels of employment, production and real income. (3) To promote exchange stability. (4) To assist in the establishment of a multilateral system of payments for current transactions and to eliminate foreign exchange restrictions, which hamper the growth of world trade. (5) To give confidence to members by making the resources of the Fund temporarily available to them under adequate safeguards. (6) To shorten the duration and lessen the degree of disequilibrium in members' international balances of payments.

The highest authority of the Fund is exercised by the Board of Governors. Each member of the Fund elects a governor and an alternate. Most of the governors' powers are delegated to a smaller group of 22 executive directors. A further group of governors known as the Interim Committee, established in 1974, meet about twice a year to review world economic conditions and the activities of the Fund.

Quotas

Each Fund member pays a quota expressed in special drawing rights (SDRs) and fixed at the time of joining. The quota reflects economic size and other factors, and is reviewed every five years. Members generally pay the quota in 75% of their own currency and in 25% of reserve assets such as gold or foreign currencies. Quotas determine voting power, which is a sore point with countries whose large populations are in inverse ratio to their share of world trade.

Special drawing rights

These were created in 1969 under the first amendment of the articles. Fears were then expressed about the adequacy of international liquidity (money available for financing balance of payments deficits). It was hoped eventually to make SDRs the principal reserve asset of the international monetary system. The value of the SDR, originally defined in terms of gold, was altered in 1981 to a weighted basket of five currencies: the United States dollar (42%), the German mark (19%), the French franc (13%), the Japanese yen (13%) and £ sterling (13%). The change led to an increasing acceptance of SDRs in the commercial and Euro-currency markets. In that year, seven major international banks in London established a market in SDR certificates of deposit. Some banks also introduced current accounts to ease the settlement of SDR transactions. Efforts have been made to establish a secondary market in SDRs, but the wide buy and sell quotations are a disadvantage to private investors and for the time being it appears that only very large amounts of SDRs will be dealt in.

Allocation of SDRs

Under the articles, the Fund may create unconditional liquidity in the form of SDR allocations to each Fund member if there is a long-term global need for reserves. Since 1970, SDRs have been allocated as follows: 1970–72 SDR 3bn a year; 1973–78 nil; 1979–81 SDR 4bn a year. The total stock of SDRs in 1983 stood at 21bn; the total quotas of the Fund, valued at SDR 61bn, were held mainly in national currencies.

Questions on international liquidity

Q1. Appraise the differing roles now played in the international monetary system by gold and special drawing rights.

A1. Until 1971, gold played a fairly important part in the international monetary system. Dollars were convertible into gold
and it was the numeraire (par value) against which other
countries fixed their exchange rates. When used for transactions
with central banks it had an official fixed price, but there was also
a free market price for gold. It became more and more difficult to
keep two separate prices for gold, especially when speculation
drove the free market price above the official price. In 1971, the
United States gave up the convertibility of the dollar and fixed
rates made way for floating rates.

Because of the huge increase in the free market price of gold,
alterations were made in IMF rules to allow members to value
their gold holdings at the market instead of the official price.
Efforts were made to demonetise gold (abolish gold from the
international monetary system). In 1976 the IMF abandoned the
official gold price and sold one sixth of its gold to finance aid for
developing countries; one sixth was returned to member
countries. By 1977, the proportion of gold held by member
countries of the IMF had fallen to 15% of their total reserves,
compared with 59% in 1964. SDRs allocated in 1970, 1971 and
1972 did not take the place of gold, which is still widely held as an
international medium of exchange and a store of value. SDRs
made up even less of member countries' total reserves at 3.6%
than did gold although the 1981 allocation of SDR 4bn increased
this percentage.

The differing roles now played in the international monetary
system by gold and SDRs can be summed up as follows: gold is
no longer the lynch pin of the international monetary system as it
was during the Bretton Woods era, but it has not lost its lustre for
those countries and people who, during any monetary crisis, see
gold as the ultimate store of value. By contrast SDRs are not
regarded as a store of value, but they are gaining increasing
credence as an international medium of exchange and even more
as a unit of account. The IMF publishes daily SDR rates for about
40 currencies, some of which are also quoted on the foreign
exchange page of the *Financial Times,* and also published monthly
by the IMF in *International Financial Statistics.*

Q2. Why were special drawing rights (SDRs) introduced to the
contemporary international financial system? Do you agree that
they will eventually become the principal international reserve
asset?

A2. The idea of SDRs arose out of the IMF meeting in Rio de Janeiro in 1967. SDRs were to be an addition to the world's supply of reserve currencies. These, consisting mainly of dollars, sterling and gold, were considered inadequate for the growing volume of world trade. SDRs were approved by the 1st Amendment to the Articles of Agreement in 1968. The first distribution of £3,500m took place in 1970, and the rest of the agreed £9,500m was spread over 1971 and 1972, with the United Kingdom's allocation being £410m. A second allocation for SDR 12bn was spread over 1979–81, and the United Kingdom received £304m.

From April 1978 the IMF Articles were amended to include the objective of making the SDR 'the principal reserve asset in the international monetary system'. This aim has not been achieved. For many countries, the SDR lacks the acceptability that is the prime quality of money, national or international. They prefer gold or a convertible currency, although the SDR is becoming more widely used as a unit of account. Eurobonds were first denominated in SDRs in 1975, although payments and receipts were in United States dollars. Tolls for the Suez Canal were similarly denominated in SDRs after the Middle East war, with payment in dollars.

In spite of these minor triumphs, there seems little likelihood at present of SDRs becoming the principal international reserve asset. They lack universal acceptability; they are 'recognisable' only among a limited few; they have not the appeal or store of value quality of gold and, during international currency crises, their acceptability is likely to diminish rather than increase. As a unit of account, however, their importance is increasing. The 'basket' valuation of the SDR (five currencies) gives it a stable exchange value, even when individual currencies plunge and soar.

Q3. Describe the operations and financing of the World Bank (International Bank for Reconstruction and Development) and its subsidiaries.

A3. The World Bank began operations in 1945 with 58 members. Its first aim was to provide capital for the reconstruction of post-war Europe. It now has over 100 members and is concerned with providing resources for the developing countries. It lends only to member Governments (or those with Government guarantees). Interest is charged at market rates and loans are made only for specific, not general projects. These have included agriculture, education, water supply, transport, tourism and electricity. Technical assistance is also provided. Funds are raised by borrowing in the world's capital markets, selling participations in its loans and by placements with Governments and central banks.

The International Development Association: this was set up in 1960 as a World Bank subsidiary to provide long-term loans for up to 60 years for 'priority' projects. There may be no interest charged – only a small service charge. The idea is to delay repayment until the project is completed, when it can then be spread over its useful life. Borrowers must be Governments or backed by Governments. The loans ranged between $100m and $300m from 1961 to 1969; with $999m in 1972 and 3,341m in 1983. The percentage of loans for the poorest countries has gone up from 70%, until now almost all funds go to countries with the lowest per capita income. Capital is raised from initial subscriptions, with Part 1 (developed nations) paying less than Part 2 (developing nations), from replenishments of subscriptions, from grants from the World Bank and from participants in the sales of IDA credits.

The International Finance Corporation is a subsidiary of the World Bank, and invests up to 25% in private enterprise without Government guarantee. When the investment project concludes, the Corporation sells its equity holding to recoup its funds. Other finance comes from World Bank loans and sales of IFC loans to participants. Its significance is in its lending to *private* projects without Government guarantee and the taking up of equity, later sold, in these projects. The IFC thus encourages entrepreneurial undertakings in areas that might not otherwise be able to develop them. Its role is like that of a lender of last resort in a private capacity.

Q4. How does the International Monetary Fund obtain the funds which it makes available to member countries in balance of payments difficulties? Are the resources which it can use sufficient to meet potential demands for assistance?

A4. The IMF obtains the funds which it makes available to member countries in balance of payments difficulties mainly from its quota system. Each member gets a 'quota' based on its position in world trade, etc. The largest trading countries get the highest quota. Subscriptions have to be paid with 75% in members' own currency and 25% in another currency or SDRs. These provide the IMF with its main source of funds. Further finance came in the late 1970s from gold sales and special borrowings, including some from the developed countries and OPEC members. Supplementary facilities of around $10bn were introduced in 1979, provided mainly from the Saudi Arabian Monetary Agency, the United States and the Deutsche Bundesbank. New allocations of 4bn SDRs were also made yearly from 1979 to 1982.

The resources that the IMF can use are insufficient to meet actual and potential demands for assistance, as is proved by the fact that supplementary facilities have been devised. Countries in surplus like to remain so. Debts piled up by various developing nations have worried the lending banks, and re-scheduling of the debt is now a top priority, which the IMF has been brought in to solve. But Governments rarely put lending to the IMF or the World Bank among their top priorities, particularly at election times, and so the lending banks themselves may have to come up with a solution.

Q5. Describe sterling balances.

A5. Sterling balances were balances of sterling held in London by official holders (overseas central banks and international organisations) and private holders (commercial firms). The holdings of private sterling were very stable; official holdings were more volatile, moving out quickly whenever sterling came under pressure or increasing when sterling was strong. Such movements created difficulties for the United Kingdom because they arose from external, not internal events. The United Kingdom promised to phase out the sterling balances on joining the EEC. Earlier attempts to do so had foundered, mostly because Britain had tried to guarantee their value. With the help of the BIS a scheme was devised, by which official holders could convert their holdings into dollar-denominated medium-term bonds, or be repaid if the United Kingdom official reserves fell below a minimum agreed level.

Q6. Describe the European currency joint float (the snake).

A6. In 1972, the six original members of the EEC agreed to keep their currencies fixed at a margin of 1.125% each side of the 'central' rate with the United States dollar. Britain joined the snake but left after five weeks, and sterling began floating in June. Other members came and went, some more than once. Sweden was a member for a short time, until eventually the 'survivors' numbered Belgium, Denmark, Germany, Holland, Luxemburg and Norway. The main reasons for the snake's comparative lack of success were the differing rates of inflation, interest and growth in the countries concerned, and their inability or unwillingness to accept the disciplines of a fixed exchange rate. (However, the lessons learned were put to good use in the creation of the European Monetary System, which came into force in March 1980.)

Q7. What strains were imposed on the international banking system over the period 1973–5 by the great increase in the price of oil?

A7. Any large international movement of funds (hot money) creates problems for banks. So does any sudden increase or decrease of the price, or change in the demand and supply conditions of any vital resource used internationally. The major strain imposed on the international banking system over the years 1973–5 was the problem of recycling funds. OPEC countries earned large surpluses. Most of these surpluses were deposited in dollars in United States banks, sterling in United Kingdom banks and Eurodollars in banks of other countries. This money was often short-term and thus very volatile. However, borrowers of large amounts usually want long-term loans. The dichotomy between short-term deposits and long-term loans creates a problem for the international banks concerned. Furthermore, as the deposits from OPEC countries were large in relation to other deposits, the ratio of capital and reserves to deposits was reduced to a level that could not always be regarded as prudent.

Another strain on international banks caused by the oil price increase was the fact that for banks taking in other currencies (e.g., a British bank accepting Eurodollar deposits) there was often no lender of last resort facility. The deposit-accepting bank could not so easily lend in those currencies whose central bank was inaccessible in terms of the required funds. Standby facilities were often arranged between the international banks to attempt to solve these problems. The strains were, in effect, the same as for the smallest banks and arose from the same cause: the choice between liquidity and profitability. The only real difference for the international banks was that the sums involved were vastly greater so that the problems were magnified.

Q8. Describe the role and assess the significance of the Bank for International Settlements.

A8. The Bank for International Settlements was set up in 1930 in Basle, Switzerland. It is an organisation of central banks and the directors meet in Basle every month. Its first objectives were to carry out the reparations settlements of the First World War under the Dawes and Young plans. In 1931 the Hoover moratorium suspended reparation payments and for a time the future of the BIS looked somewhat insecure, although it continued to give financial assistance to central banks. Austria, Hungary and Yugoslavia received this help in 1931; the United Kingdom in 1977 when trying to phase out the sterling balances, as well as on other occasions in the previous twenty years.

The BIS had acted as fiscal agent for the Universal Postal Union and the European iron and steel community and was therefore in a favourable position to be the agent for the EEC's short-term support mechanism. This role was heightened when the European Monetary System was adopted. The BIS became the agent for the European Monetary Co-operation Fund. It carried out the EMCF's functions, which were recording the accounts transactions of central banks when they intervened in EEC currencies to provide short-term support. The BIS monitors the Eurocurrency short-term market, providing authoritative data. It co-operates with the IMF and provides a meeting and discussion place for international monetary problems. Its balance sheet is expressed in gold Swiss francs and its total assets are over $20,000bn with 98% of its deposits from central banks.

Index

117